We Hold These Truths to Be Self-Evident

The National Guard and the Categorical Imperative

Anne C. Armstrong, J.D., D.L.S.

National Guard Educational Foundation;
National Guard Memorial Museum, Library, and Archive

Series in American History

VERNON PRESS

www.vernonpress.com

In the Americas:	*In the rest of the world:*
Vernon Press	Vernon Press
1000 N West Street, Suite 1200	C/Sancti Espiritu 17,
Wilmington, Delaware, 19801	Malaga, 29006
United States	Spain

Series in American History

Library of Congress Control Number: 2021936403

ISBN: 978-1-64889-374-2

Also available: 978-1-64889-148-9 [Hardback]; 978-1-64889-272-1 [PDF, E-Book]

Cover design by Vernon Press. Cover figure designed by alejo_m / Freepik.

Contents

Abstract

This book makes the ethical case for a volunteer Citizen-Soldier military in a democratic republic using Immanuel Kant's (1724-1804) Categorical Imperative as justification. An Enlightenment theory, Kant's Categorical Imperative represents a higher moral duty-free from reliance upon consequence. The Categorical Imperative directs that a moral law fit three requirements: the action must be universally applicable, deemed as fair by all parties to the action, and not use men as a means to an end. By reviewing the history of the National Guard of the United States, I draw the reader away from a traditional Utilitarian argument of cost/benefit analysis and demonstrate that the Deontological argument is equally applicable. National Guard history is relevant because the Citizen-Soldier military in the United States has evolved over 400 years. Beginning with the first legislated Muster in 1636, pre-Enlightenment village bands protected the tiny, immigrant communities, today volunteer Citizen-Soldiers stand shoulder-to-shoulder with their career counterparts in both domestic and foreign theaters. While the Utilitarian based cost/benefit analysis changes over time with circumstances, I demonstrate that the Categorical Imperative applies throughout the National Guard's long, complicated history.

The procedure used to make the argument follows the history of the United States in chronological order. In each chapter, a significant leader is looked at closely – how that person reflected the Categorical Imperative over the changes in the National Guard from the First Muster in 1636 to present day. Specifically, we look at the birth of the nation with General George Washington, the turbulent nineteenth century to World War One with Senator Charles Dick (R-OH), and the post-modern era of the 1940s through the early twenty-first century with Generals Ellard A. Walsh and Frank Grass. By evaluating world events and these remarkably influential men, we observe the Categorical Imperative in action as it shapes the National Guard and reflects the Enlightenment principles upon with the nation was founded. In conclusion, the reader will see that Kant's theory of a higher moral duty – one that results in a universal law of fairness and non-manipulation of one's fellow man as a means to an end – does, in fact, readily apply to the Citizen-Soldier concept in a democratic republic such as the United States.

Short Statement on Development of Subject

This book is an adapted version of my dissertation for the Doctor of Liberal Studies Program at Georgetown University in Washington, D. C. As the Director of the National Guard Memorial Museum, Library, and Archive, I am the lead historian for the National Guard Association of the United States. I find I spend the majority of my time hearing the Utilitarian argument for the continued service of the National Guard of the United States. During my studies at Georgetown, I was exposed to Immanuel Kant's normative arguments and realized that American voluntary military service goes much deeper than mere "bang for the buck". There is something to the idea that, born of the Enlightenment, the Founding Fathers realized Americans understood the timeless need to protect their communities. Since this argument is timeless, I set out to make the argument span the entire 400-year history of the National Guard and to show how it succeeded in some ways and failed in others.

Acronyms

AGAUS	Adjutants General Association of the United States
AGR	Active Guard and Reserve
ATF	Bureau of Alcohol, Tobacco, Firearms, and Explosives
CCC	Civilian Conservation Corps
CNGB	Chief, National Guard Bureau
DHS	Department of Homeland Security
ESGR	Employer Support of the Guard and Reserve
FEMA	Federal Emergency Management Agency
GWOT	Global War on Terror
JSPS	Joint Strategic Planning System
NATO	North Atlantic Treaty Organization
NORAD	North American Aerospace Defense Command
NORTHCOM	Northern Command
ODS/S	Operations Desert Shield and Storm
OEF	Operation Enduring Freedom
OIF	Operation Iraqi Freedom
SPP	State Partnership Program
UMT	Universal Military Training
WPA	Works Progress Administration

Dedicated with sincere gratitude to the staff of the National Guard Educational Foundation.

Introduction

Two seemingly unrelated but critical events occurred during the seventeenth century that form the basis of this book. First, small bands of militia in pre-Colonial America formed, based on decisions made by community legislatures, to protect the interests of the vulnerable villages. Second, the era known as the Enlightenment began in Western Europe. The man credited with coining the name of the era, Immanuel Kant (1724-1804), was born in Königsburg, Germany soon after the turn of the century. The militias would go on over four hundred years to evolve into the modern National Guard of the United States. Immanuel Kant would systematize the nature of moral duty into a universal theory, arguably immune to change over time, and a fundamental tenet of human society.

The issue at hand is whether Kant's universal "Categorical Imperative" can be applied to service in the militias from 1636 to present day. This book lays the groundwork and sets examples through 400 years of history to demonstrate that Kant's imperative holds up and applies as an ideal to voluntary military service. This book is based on the author's doctoral thesis in the Humanities at Georgetown University in Washington, D.C. Critical to this argument is that the United States was founded upon the Enlightenment theory that authority is granted to the legislatures from the governed and not the reverse. Kant's Categorical Imperative provides a fairly complex system to determine the behavior of men employing an "ought to" formulation. Rather than looking at hypothetical imperatives in which one conditions the goal and action to attain it within an "if" statement like "if I want a cup of coffee, I make it in the coffee pot", Kant addressed a Categorical Imperative – one that is not based on consequence but upon universal duty. For example, a Kantian imperative would be: "I ought not to lie". There are no conditions or consequences attached to this admonition.

The history of this argument is an interesting one – primarily because it has been largely ignored. During the period of time that the National Guard found itself fighting for its existence in the halls of the nation's capital, John Stuart Mill (1806-1873) and Jeremy Bentham (1748-1832) formulated the moral doctrine of Utilitarianism. The several state legislatures of the United States found this argument seductive and used it to justify the use of their individual military forces rather than the less calculating lines of the Kantian Categorical Imperative. Much later, President Dwight D. Eisenhower (1890-1969) coined the very Utilitarian phrase "more bang for the buck" that beautifully illustrates how wedded both the Federal Government and senior military leadership came to the Utilitarian argument. Because the Kantian argument has been widely ignored by scholars and advocates, this book is written to fill that void.

The Categorical Imperative has been in action in United States military service since the nation's inception. The book is designed, chapter-by-chapter, to show how it has applied over time in the development of the nation. In the fledgling pre-colonial United States of the seventeenth century, village legislatures began to see a need for local defense. The legislature, elected by the village men, ordered certain citizens to serve in the local militia. Through representative government, the citizens themselves directed this service. Per Kant's (as yet unformed) Categorical Imperative, this voluntary service model was based on the ideal that men "ought" to serve to protect their community and its interests. Over time, as the world changed and the United States formed into a global superpower, the universality of the Categorical Imperative still applied. By World War II, recently enfranchised African American citizens in New York, Washington, DC, and other areas on the East Coast, volunteered with state National Guard units to go overseas to fight with career Army peers in a war against the Third Reich of Germany. With growing freedom and ability to assimilate into society, African Americans left the United States to fight overseas hoping that integration in the military might influence their integration in American society at home. These two simple examples demonstrate the universality over time of the Categorical Imperative as volunteers performed a duty to protect their communities. In the first example, the villagers protected their families and their own plots of land, while in the second example, citizens volunteered to protect national interests overseas. The world changed but the Categorical Imperative remained stalwart.

This book will show that the Categorical Imperative, as it relates to the Citizen-soldier concept of military service in the United States is an ideal not always attained. However, in application, the theory applies across different historical periods and this is demonstrated through a discussion of its application to voluntary military service in various events and contexts within the United States from 1636 to the present day. The following chapters will show how, in a democratic republic, the concept of voluntary military service based on a Citizen-soldier model conforms elegantly to Kant's Categorical Imperative.

Chapter I

Setting the Stage.

The Citizen-soldier: A Normative Perspective on Military Service in the United States of America.

The official birthday of the National Guard of the United States is December 13th, 1636. In the small village of Salem, Massachusetts, the rudimentary legislature announced that all able-bodied men, ages 16 to 60, would be required to form a basic military regiment in order to defend Salem from all hostile attackers. The men were identified by name, a hierarchy with formal rank proposed, and a date and location identified for a Muster. Thus, the first American Militia was born.[1] The standing Army of the United States, not to exist for another 150 years or so, started in Massachusetts by relying on the local villagers to respond to mutual threat and need to survive. The original settlers brought with them the social structure and concept of military service from Western Europe where the influence of Enlightenment thought was beginning to hold sway. Seventeenth-century European society included community interdependence in day-to-day economic, religious, and military life – in which authority of governance rose from the individuals to the appointed legislature rather than fell from a divine monarchy to his subjects. Thus, authority for the defense of the community was recognized by the community as part of the social contract. As early as the mid-seventeenth Century, this social contract began to take form specifically in the writings of such philosophers like Thomas Hobbes (1588-1679) and John Locke (1632-1704). Discoveries in science, a reliance on Reason, and a new understanding of human dignity enforced the idea that responsible citizenship included mutual defense brought about by mutual need. In this book, I will argue that, while the Citizen-soldier concept is the best operational model for a modern democratic republic, it is also the most fitting moral and ethical model. The form of mutual defense taken by the early

---

[1] Nathaniel B. Shurtleff, ed., *Records of the Governor and Company of the Massachusetts Bay of New England*, Vol. I, 1628-1641 (Boston: Press of William White, 1853), 186-187.

militias in the colonies is a common method and benefits from a Deontological analysis. Therefore, I will discuss Immanuel Kant's (1724-1804) ethical theory as the basis for an argument that the citizen-soldier model is a critical and ethically applicable version of military service in a democratic republic such as the United States of America.

Before beginning a discussion of the roots of the colonial Militia and Kantian ethical theory, however, a brief history of military war theory is appropriate. The most famous analysis of war theory with relevance to Kant harkens back to St. Augustine (354-430), living in North Africa and Italy. The moral basis of a just war, explained St. Augustine in *City of God, Book XIX*, was to wage war in order to seek peace. War could be justified in order to retain property or safety of one's own community (property, life, liberty). Further adapted by St. Thomas Aquinas (1225-1274), the doctrine of a Just War developed into a series of logical choices – a war must have a legitimate purpose, be waged by legitimate authority, and be motivated by peaceful intentions.[2] In 1977, Michael Walzer refined the history of Just War Theory in his classic book *Just and Unjust Wars*. However, the doctrine of Just War is a pitfall easily fallen into by the reader of this book. This book does not set out to argue the nature of Just War Theory but, rather, to argue that the nature of the specific service of the Citizen-soldier can be established as a performance of Kant's Categorical Imperative. There is no question raised about Just War and the nature of warfare itself. This book focuses on the nature of the citizen as a part-time soldier and his military service on a local, state, and national level in a democratic republic.

The original European settlers of the North American continent as far back as 1607 fled Great Britain and Western Europe for two fundamental reasons: religious freedom and economic adventure. At first, the conditions they encountered in the New World left them ill-equipped for survival and the earliest settlements failed. By 1636, however, the established colonies and their local communities had begun to thrive. Along with the Western European religions and merchant traditions came all the social, economic, and cultural accoutrements that such immigrants inherently bring. For protection, they brought with them the concept of the seventeenth-century Militia tradition. For education, they brought with them the concept of the seventeenth-century University. Harvard (1636), William & Mary (1693), and Yale (1701) were all founded within a few years of each other in the original colonies of Massachusetts, Virginia, and Connecticut respectively. Continuing into the eighteenth century, the first three were soon followed by the University of

---

[2] St. Thomas Aquinas, *Summa Theologiae*, trans. Fathers of the English Dominican Province (Online Edition: 2017), question 40: War, art. 1, accessed April 10, 2019, http://www.newadvent.org/summa/3040.htm#article1

Pennsylvania (1740), the University of Delaware (1743), and New Jersey's Princeton in 1746. The significance of higher education in the Colonies is that it provided a popular venue for the dissemination of current philosophical thought.

The colonists were careful to bring their culture with them to these new institutions – and that meant bringing the Enlightenment. While an exact date of the beginning of the Enlightenment is impossible to specify, it is critical to acknowledge that the philosophical thought migrated from Western Europe with the early colonists along with commercial trade and pursuit of religious freedom. Interestingly, Thomas Jefferson (1743-1826) had a summary of Kant's philosophy in his prodigious personal library.[3] starting with the Enlightenment tenet that primary authority rests in the people, who then form the basis of legitimate government, we can see a clear Kantian application to militia service in the colonies of the eighteenth century.[4] Immanuel Kant, whose life spanned the eighteenth century, developed his philosophy at first with an analysis of Pure Reason.[5] He was particularly interested in what the new sciences were able to explain based on the phenomenological world – that which is in front of us – and the numerological world – that which has a reality unto itself. However, he felt that Ethics could only be applied by a sense of Practical Reason. To that end, he wrote *A Critique of Practical Reason* (1788) and *The Metaphysics of Morals* (1797). In these volumes, he concluded that ethics rely on a universal and timeless sense of duty. This sense of duty does not take temporal circumstances or consequences into account. The Deontological argument can be distilled to three requirements. First, it is a universal duty that must apply to all people. Second, its execution must not use men as a means to an end, and finally, the parties involved must deem the behavior as fair. Kant's Deontological ethic exists independently of the consequences of one's actions, does not change over time, and may be applied as a law. Once a duty is realized, then it exists forever in the past, present, and future. Such a duty that meets these criteria and creates a sense of "ought" is known as a Categorical Imperative.

> And so categorical imperatives are possible by this: that the idea of freedom makes me a member of an intelligible world, and consequently, if I were only this, all my actions *would* always be in conformity with the

[3] Charles Francois Dominique de Villers, *Philosophie de Kant* (Metz: chez Collignon, 1801). De Villers volume may be viewed in Jefferson's library via the Internet at: accessed May 15, 2018, http://lcweb2.loc.gov/cgi-bin/ampage?collId=rbc3&fileName=rbc0001_2007jeffcat2page.db&recNum=60.
[4] Natural Law as defined by John Locke (1632-1704) and David Hume (1711-1776).
[5] Kant published *Critique of Pure Reason* seven years earlier in 1781.

autonomy of the will; but since at the same time I intuit myself as a member of the world of sense, they *ought* to be in conformity with it; and this *categorical* ought represents a synthetic proposition a priori, since to my will affected by sensible desires there is added the idea of the same will but belonging to the world of the understanding – a will pure and practical of itself, which contains the supreme condition, in accordance with reason, of the former will....[6]

Almost in parallel, Jeremy Bentham (1748-1832) set forth an alternate ethical theory that was elaborated by John Stuart Mill (1806-1873). Utilitarianism, rather than depending on a universal higher duty, relied (and continues to rely) on causes of action and their consequences. Its fundamental concept is that mankind's goal is the attainment of happiness and what benefits the most people must be the correct, ethical choice of action. By dispensing with concern over cost or benefit, Kant's Deontological method of determination of ethical behavior directly contradicts Bentham's and Mill's. While Utilitarianism relies almost entirely on the consequences of the action taken, Kant's universal duty remains stubbornly indifferent to consequences entirely. In the case of the history of the National Guard of the United States, however, the use of both seemingly contradictory theories may be surprisingly advantageous. When one considers the benefits to the nation of a less expensive force because of its part-time nature, then one is considering the "utility" of the service. The fact that most National Guardsmen come directly from the community they serve makes their commutes shorter and cheaper. The National Guard is a Utilitarian philosopher's ideal. Such a cost/benefit analysis is absolutely critical to the statisticians in the Pentagon as they go to Capitol Hill to ask for budgetary considerations. However, for a discussion of the sense of duty to serve one's community, the best philosophical test to turn to is Kant's Deontological one. While it is clear to the statisticians in the Pentagon that a Utilitarian argument for the National Guard is a successful one, the voluntary nature of the Guard and the sense of duty to protect one's own community allows for a Deontological argument. In all voluntary military service, the citizen-soldier must be self-motivated by a duty to society as a whole to serve in a military force that is asking for his potential death and his willingness to kill on its behalf – the stakes are just that high. Simply explaining that it is cheaper and drill pay is worth the sacrifice may be insufficient to motivate the volunteer. As additional motivation, Kant's "higher duty" reasons that such service in the

---

[6] Immanuel Kant, *The Cambridge Edition of the Works of Immanuel Kant: Practical Philosophy*, gen. eds. Paul Guyer and Allan W. Wood, ed. and trans. Mary J. Gregor (New York: Cambridge University Press, 2008), 100-1.

defense of the community protects the soldier's interests as well as those of his neighbors. In the case of the higher duty, such service protects one's own interests, can be expected of one's neighbor in return, and is fairly extended to all – not just a conscripted few. In order to protect the community by those who know it best, the citizenry "ought" to recognize a universal duty to serve, that it is a fair commitment, and that – by virtue of mutual benefit – no one is used as a means to an end. This circumstance is a rare time that both Utilitarianism and Deontology can be the basis of a valid argument in support of the same goal.

At this point, I feel it is important to note the significance of the Deontological argument on behalf of service in a citizen-soldier military in a democratic republic versus the Utilitarian argument. It is unique, I believe, that both can work in parallel when supporting this type of service. However, it is equally important to recognize that the nature of Utilitarianism relies heavily on circumstances and the resulting consequences of actions based on those circumstances. Therefore, Utilitarianism is teleological and can re-enforce a cost/benefit analysis at one time that, as circumstances change, becomes counter-enforcing. In other words, at one point the cost/benefit analysis may favor of citizen-solder force while at another point in time, the cost/benefit analysis may not favor a citizen-soldier force. In one set of circumstances, the National Guard may be cheaper and more efficient, while in another set it may be more expensive and less efficient than other alternatives. This fact is a weakness in the otherwise perfectly valid Utilitarian argument. On the other hand, Kant's Categorical Imperative, by definition, is universal and timeless. If the Categorical Imperative applies favorably to citizen-soldier service in one set of circumstances, it must always apply in all circumstances. That is exactly what I hope to prove and what makes it a more convincing argument than Utilitarianism on behalf of the nature of service in the National Guard of the United States.

While the Deontological sense of duty is universal and timeless, what does change is the historical series of circumstances and events to which one applies the Deontological argument. In the case of military duty in a democratic republic such as the National Guard of the United States, the national story certainly evolves through contingencies, wars, natural disasters, civil disorders, administrations, and times of peace – while the duty to serve remains unchanging. This book, therefore, will apply the normative argument for the citizen-soldier model in the United States by examining it in relation to significant events and eras in American history. By reiterating the three-prong requirements of Kant's normative theory of ethics, I mean to stress that the concept of the American citizen-soldier involves fairness, universality, and the use of the individual in the service to the community other than as a means to an end. Although this application may not have been overtly intentional, the universal nature of Kant's Deontology renders that aspect moot. As will be discussed in great length throughout this book, over the course of centuries, the Kantian concept of the Categorical Imperative does not change significantly if at all. Following the post-Colonial era, the self-reliance and independence presented by the nineteenth-century American Transcendentalists and the modern Pragmatists continue to support the Kantian theory of a greater duty of service with an emphasis on respect for the rights of the citizen to a non-military life.[7]

With the advent of World War One and World War Two, however, we see a great shift in philosophy to the Post-Modern despair that results from the capacity for systemic mass annihilation and its execution in the wars. While the nation looks to create a stronger federal force to address the threat of Communism during the Cold War, the National Guard argues that it can bear the burden. The Categorical Imperative holds sway. The National Guard of the 1960s and 1970s, however, is an example of the failure of the leadership in the United States and within the National Guard to uphold the Kantian methodology. During the '60s and '70s the United States intentionally leaves the Guard out of the Vietnam War and the negative public reaction is dramatic. Military theory (to leave the Guard behind) and Kantian ethical theory diverge with terrible results. In this case, the Lyndon B. Johnson Administration determined that the containment of Communism in Southeast Asia needed to be subtle and removed from the public eye back home in the United States. From a Kantian perspective, the inequality between those men who were sent to Vietnam and those who were not becomes an ethical problem rather than the mutual protection and defense of the community (or, in this case, the nation.) In the case of American involvement in Vietnam, the deferments from the draft and the draft system itself result in the *de facto* failure to apply the Kantian Categorical Imperative – the draft was not universal, appeared decidedly unfair, and treated men as a means to an end. Selective service during this era was not universal but determined to use only specific individuals for deployment. Then, by allowing the exceptions to the rule of the draft (the deferments) to exist even those selected were winnowed down to fewer and the men who could not meet the deferment criteria were sent into combat. Not only was the Vietnam draft system particular, the deferments appear to have been unfairly distributed to those of means, power, and wealth. Such deferment criteria included being

---

[7] Here, the Transcendental importance placed on self-reliance alone may even account for the validity of conscientious objection. Emphasis will particularly be placed on Ralph Waldo Emerson (1803-1882), Henry David Thoreau (1817-1862), and William James (1842-1910).

enrolled in Divinity school, having an occupation in agriculture, having an occupation stipulated by law as deferrable, hardship, deferrable medical conditions, and qualifying as an official deferred by law. By the time the draftee filtered through the list only a certain type of candidate remained; the unemployed, the uneducated, those unable to craft a hardship appeal, or those not appointed in official capacities. Lastly, such a drafting system used the vulnerable draftee merely as a body to fill a quota – or, in other words, as a means to an end. During the 1960s and '70s, the people of the United States witnessed the utter corruption of the Kantian ethic – the seemingly unfair selection of draftees, at the expense of those who were wealthy or connected enough to avoid the draft through the deferment process. When only the poor, uneducated, and unable to meet deferment requirements are sent to war thousands of miles away, the impression is clearly that they are being used as cannon fodder – a fate avoided by the more advantaged young men. The draft procedures represented highly selective, unfair treatment as well as using men as a means to an end.

The last straw of the breakdown of trust between a democratic republic and its self-sacrificing military citizen-soldiers came in May, 1970, when four student protesters were killed by National Guardsmen at Kent State University in Ohio. Symptomatic of the frustration brought about by racial inequity and resentment, the National Guard was used repeatedly in the domestic civil disorder after the post-Civil Rights Act of 1964. Not immune to race riots before the Civil Rights Act of 1964, the Oklahoma National Guard famously confronted the issue in 1921 in Tulsa. From 1964-1968, ghastly race riots broke out around the country – so striking that historians named the period, "The Long, Hot Summers". On each occasion, the National Guard was utilized by the local legislatures to help contain the violence and damage caused by rioting in the streets. Particular destruction happened in Watts, CA, Detroit, MI, Newark, NJ, Washington, DC, and Baltimore, MD. Unlike service in Vietnam, however, the Kantian ethic can be found applied on the urban streets of America. The citizen-soldiers, those who knew their own communities the best, came to serve and protect their communities. Citizen-soldiers had an organic understanding of their service, they treated the local population as fairly as they could under duress, and no one was used as a means to an end. When the soldier protected the local butcher's from being burned, he was supporting his own neighborhood and protecting his own interests as well as those of the community.

Following the end of the Vietnam War, which resulted in the United States admitting military defeat for the first time in its history, the National Guard, led by its general officers and high-level enlisted corps, had to be rehabilitated by its leadership to rebuild its credibility and restructure itself. From 1973 to the early 1980s, the National Guard returned to its primary mission of domestic support in times of natural and man-made disasters. In the early '80s, the Guard supported such small contingencies as the liberation of Granada and the removal of Manuel Noriega from Panama. In 1990, President George H. W. Bush deployed more than 75,000 National Guard troops to support Operations Desert Shield and Storm. The soldiers knew that they were the vanguard of what was called "the Vietnam hangover" -- they were to be supported and applauded for their service. This First Gulf War broke the overcast of what had been a cloud over the American military – both the active duty and the Citizen-soldier. Following this service and its successful end, the National Guard next found itself supporting the American mission in the former Yugoslavia in the mid and late '90s under President Clinton. By the time the mission ended, the National Guard had deployed approximately 7,000 troops to the Balkans. The National Guard fully returned to its role as the citizen-soldier in comportment with the original Kantian sense of duty to serve one's community and country. Like World War One and World War Two, though the service took place overseas on behalf of a country other than the United States, the mission was clear and voluntary. From a Kantian perspective, citizen-soldiers were not only serving their own communities voluntarily as a higher duty but also serving the global community.

September 11, 2001, changed everything with regard to U.S. military policy but it didn't change the ethical duty embodied by the National Guard of the United States. If anything, it enhanced it. Suddenly, on one clear day in the early fall, the National Guard was called upon to do its mission in the local community as it had never been asked to before – and, within days, to deploy its troops thousands of miles away to perform its mission alongside the active duty in a remote, unfamiliar country. Demand for the National Guard doubled while the mission and the ethical justification for the citizen-soldier remained the same. Soldiers and airmen understood the universal application of their service and sacrifice, they acknowledged their human dignity with the fairness of treatment, and no man was used as a means to an end – the mission was voluntary, singular, and well-defined. Today, these missions continue and the National Guard is still asked to serve both in war overseas and support stateside for such missions as hurricane relief, other natural disasters, and Mexican border patrol. In 2008, the Commanding General of the National Guard was authorized to wear a fourth star and commissioned as a full General Officer. This rank placed him on an equal footing with the other General Officers in command of the U.S. Army, Air Force, Marines, and Navy. In 2011, the Commanding General was appointed as a member of the Joint Chiefs of Staff and has since carved out a unique niche for the Guard – one which still rises from the 17th and eighteenth-century Enlightenment sense of ethical duty. Because that duty has withstood the test of time and truly is universal, it shows that it can hold sway during times of clear application but also withstand events as they attempt to test it beyond its limits.

Lastly, allow me to point out what this book is not. Vastly finer minds than mine have found legitimate weaknesses in Kant's ethics and I do not propose to out-think them. This book is not a pure, in-depth analysis of Kant's theory of the Categorical Imperative. This discussion is concerned with the application of Kant's ethics to a particular case – that of the unique role of the citizen-soldier in a democratic republic like the United States of America. What I intend to do is take Kant's Categorical Imperative test and apply it to the citizen-soldier model of the National Guard of the United States as the military service has evolved since the seventeenth century. This book does not purport to argue that Kant had any direct effect on the Founding Fathers or any colonists while they were forming the many militias of the colonies or the Continental Army in 1775. Kant probably was not on their minds when they wrote the Second Amendment in the Bill of Rights to the Constitution in 1789. But Kant himself was a philosopher of the Enlightenment and some would argue he was its very embodiment.[8] The ethical duty of the Categorical Imperative is timeless and what he formulated from the Enlightenment thinking must apply universally throughout time. While Kant and America may have overlapped in time but never crossed paths, Kant's theory applies anytime, anywhere.

Another limit of this book is that it involves a less in-depth analysis of the Civil War – primarily because the militias were in the vast minority and were overshadowed by both the rise of Federal Volunteers and a series of very unpopular drafts. The Kantian ethic truly is universal and it does apply throughout the Civil War. However, it is important to understand that between the War of 1812 and the Mexican Punitive War of 1846, a military force of Federal Volunteers developed and was used to augment the small US Army and the militias. These troops were not part of legislated militias but state soldiers in Federal service on long-term commitments. It is important to note that the forces in the Civil War were largely comprised of a small Federal Army and militias vastly outnumbered by Volunteers committed to relatively long terms of service. In fact, as early as July 1861, President Lincoln himself called up 500,000 Volunteers for three-year tours.[9] To augment the Volunteers, there were also several drafts of involuntary service which are outside of the scope of this book. Notably, of the limited citizen-soldier militias that did serve, the "Fighting" 69th Regiment of the New York National Guard is one of the most interesting. Therefore, while a Kantian argument based on the militias of the Civil War, both Union and Confederate, applies, the vast majority of soldiers in the Civil War

---

[8] Kant is even credited with naming it an age of "enlightenment" calling it *aufklärung* in 1784.

[9] Michael Doubler, *Civilian in Peace, Soldier in War* (Lawrence: University of Kansas Press, 2003), 103.

were Volunteers, not legislated militias. In fact, after the Civil War, enrollment in the military all but disappeared – the soldiers being weary of the fight.

Finally, I must add that the Deontological argument presented here does not defend the idea of a modern local, community-based, non-legislated militia bent on vigilante justice. The Militia of which I speak in this book rests firmly in the concept of authority granted through legislation created by a representative form of government. The formal body that authorizes the formation of a militia force must be duly elected by the people – authority for military service must rise from the people to the government they elect. This is a critical differentiation – by 1903, the local militias were so legislated that the Dick Act expressly enforced an emulation of the regular Army in pay, training, equipment, intelligence, and mission. By the twenty-first century, the implementation of the Total Force Policy now renders the two services (the National Guard of the United States and the regular army) practically indistinguishable.

I have already mentioned the unique nature of service in the National Guard that allows both a Utilitarian argument as well as the Deontological one. Because the Pentagon delights in using statistics, and a Utilitarian cost/benefit analysis rests heavily on those calculations – that argument is made routinely on Capitol Hill when pursuing budgetary consideration. While that is the case, I have never heard an argument made that, not only is National Guard service efficient, it is also the "Right" thing to do for our citizens in a democratic republic. I would like to be the first to make that point; and I intend to do so here in the next few hundred pages. Therefore, there will be little to no discussion of Utilitarianism in my own argument. The Pentagon has that well in hand. To be clear: this book will apply the three pronged-test of Kant's Categorical Imperative as a timeless and universal duty to military service in the United States as the country evolved from a loosely connected set of colonies to a tightly cohesive super power of the twenty-first century. Specifically, I argue that the requirements of the Categorical Imperative render the citizen-soldier model of the National Guard the best method of military service in a democratic republic such as the United States from 1636 to the present and into the future. Along the way, the self-sacrifice, heroism, strengths, and weaknesses inherent in any endeavor involving humanity should alternately entertain, amuse, dismay, appall, surprise, and hopefully inspire the reader to revisit their faith in the Great Experiment that is the United States of America.[10]

---

[10] Finally, this book is not a recruiting tool – I do not want the reader to race off and join up at their nearest recruiting office or to sit back and wistfully think of opportunities lost because they are too old to sign up and charge San Juan Hill with Teddy Roosevelt.

Chapter II

Immanuel Kant's (1724-1804) Categorical Imperative and the National Guard of the United States (1636-2019)

Article One, Section 8 of the Constitution of the United States

"The Congress shall have Power to....Provide for organizing, arming, and disciplining, the Militia, and for governing such Part of them as may be employed in the Service of the United States...."[1]

The Second Amendment to the Constitution of the United States

"A well-regulated Militia, being necessary to the security of a free State, the right of the people to keep and bear Arms, shall not be infringed."[2]

Historically, the citizens of the United States have served dutifully in the military during times of conflict. In fact, some version of the National Guard has taken part in every conflict the United States has entered since the first Europeans landed on the shores of North America. Throughout the evolution of the US from rudimentary settlements, to colonies, to a fledgling international participant in world events, to Global Superpower, the idea of the citizen serving in the common defense has been present. The foundation of this service and the concept of a higher sense of duty came to the United States early – in the same manner, it came to the rest of the Western world but with time lost for transit across the Atlantic Ocean. This second chapter will ground the reader with an appreciation for the history of the citizen-soldier concept in America, the Enlightenment, and Immanuel Kant's Categorical Imperative In these first few pages, the reader will learn about Kant's "higher duty" and appreciation of free will as well as experience a brief history of the National Guard of the United States. This narrative is necessary to place the nexus

---

[1] US Constitution, art. 1, sec. 8, cl. 14.
[2] Ibid., amend. 2

between the Categorical Imperative and the calling to service in the method of the National Guard; one that instills the need to defend one's community while acknowledging the human rights of individuality, privacy, and pursuit of one's own ideals.

Embedded within the Declaration of Independence and the Constitution of the United States, we find clear Enlightenment concepts. Very briefly, the Enlightenment, a term coined by Immanuel Kant (1724-1804), is the name used to describe the period of time that spanned from the seventeenth century and the eighteenth century. Enlightenment scholars emphasized reason, science, the rights of the individual, and rationality. Arguably, the Enlightenment produced one of the most fertile periods of time in the intellectual history of human civilization. The most significant moral theory, for our purposes, was the Categorical Imperative – a higher sense of duty brought into clear light by Immanuel Kant in *The Metaphysics of Morals* and *The Critique of Practical Reason*. Kant was born in Königsburg, Germany. As a student of the writing of Sir Isaac Newton (1642-1727) and political theorists like Jean-Jacques Rousseau (1712-1778), Kant's philosophy was steeped in the theory that moral behavior should be rooted in self-legislation. While formulating what he called Pure Reason, Kant presumed that Pure Reason was an unattainable goal – a focus on the numinological world. As opposed to the phenomenological, tangible world, the numinological world dealt with the intangibles like beauty, love, and faith. When he delved into Practical Reason he proposed to give man a methodology that was realistically able to apply to everyday life, or the phenomenal. The maxims became a set of rules to live by and could be addressed based on situation and circumstances.

> Practical reason is in general defined as that which determines rules for the faculty of desire and will …. [and] is necessarily understood in relation to moral considerations, and these in terms of a moral law that is taken to have an unconditional Imperative force that implies that is addressed to us as sensible beings with an absolutely free capacity to choose (*Willkür*) to will or not to will to act for their sake.[3]

Balancing practical reason and self-will, Kant arrived at the Categorical Imperative – an end-stage maxim upon which circumstances had no effect.[4] To qualify as one of Kant's Categorical Imperatives, the rule had to meet three criteria – it had to be universally applicable, it had to be deemed as fair to all

---

[3] Robert Audi, ed., *The Cambridge Dictionary of Philosophy, 3rd Edition* (New York: Cambridge University Press, 2000), 551.
[4] Ibid., 555. Also known, confusingly, as *pure* Practical Reason.

participants involved in the action, and it had to clearly not use men as a means to an end. If all three prongs of the requirements were met, Kant's theory said, then the Categorical Imperative held sway and a universal law of behavior was created. When acknowledging free will in this manner, there is a double act – not only in the instance of the effect of the Categorical Imperative but in the acceptance of the universal law itself.

It is upon Kant's theory of the Categorical Imperative (the higher law) that the moral argument in this treatise hinges: that the National Guard of the United States represents the most ethical method of service in a democratic republic. Therefore, with no insult intended to an educated audience, it stands to reason that a brief synopsis of the history of the National Guard of the United States from the very outset is in order.[5] In all its forms, the existence of the National Guard spans over four hundred years and cannot possibly be contained in a single chapter with any in-depth granularity. However, an historical narrative is not the goal here – my goal is to argue that the "duty" to provide for the common defense inspired in the citizens of the nation over time is relatively unchanging and served in the past as now to create a formidable fighting force. The Kantian concept of the Categorical Imperative was and is alive and well in the citizen-soldiers of the United States National Guard.

The story begins with the Magna Carta signed by King John of England on the 15th of June, 1215. Having lost the support of the Parliament and the Church, King John was forced to abdicate power to "all free men". Represented by the Parliament that was granted the power of the purse strings, the power of "free men" existed as proof that the King was not above the law but must answer to the will of the people. Therefore, said the Magna Carta, the power to govern arises from the authority vested in the citizens and is not granted from the sovereign to his or her subjects. With such power vested in the people came the right to protect their own lives, their property, and the pursuit of their own liberty. It states:

> No free man shall be seized or imprisoned, or stripped of his rights or possessions, or outlawed or exiled, or deprived of his standing in any other way, nor will we proceed with force against him, or send others to

---

[5] Over the course of a 400-year history, terms for the various forms of armies of the United States have had different names. For consistency and clarity, the Continental Army that became the Army of the United States will be referred to as the "Continental Army" (or some obvious variation), "Standing Army" or "Regulars" (1775-1945); then, as the "Active Duty" (Post WW2 – present.) The National Guard will be referred to as Militia (1636-1865) and subsequently as National Guard. The Air Force and Air National Guard (1947) will be referred to by their two distinct names.

do so, except by the lawful judgement of his equals or by the law of the land. To no one will we sell, to no one deny or delay right or justice.[6]

The concept of Magna Carta, embedded in the previous quote, emphasized the Natural Right of the individual to protection of their property and an inherent right to personal justice. This right arose from the people and was no longer granted by a divine sovereign. In fifteenth and sixteenth-century Western Europe, this liberty and self-defense manifested itself in the Elizabethan concept of the "trayned band", a small militia force formed at the local level. The sovereign did not grant the right to protection of property to the citizenry but, quite the opposite, the citizenry inherently held the right to defend it for themselves. By virtue of establishing a clear right to individual sovereignty, the Magna Carta – in this clause – paved the way for villagers to carry the legal right and responsibility to form a local militia to protect their own property, standing, and liberty. A medieval concept, the "trayned band" was a small militia consisting of village men trained in the defense of the local community rather than an emphasis on a large, standing army. "[Queen Elizabeth I] called out the trainbands in the summer of 1588 as the Spanish Armada approached the British Isles. England would depend upon trainbands and the common militia for domestic defense until … 1661".[7] These small, well-organized groups of armed villagers were used to defend their common interests and the colloquial military-style transitioned nicely to the small settlements in Massachusetts Bay and Virginia by the sixteenth century. In Salem, MA, in December of 1636, the "trayned band" evolved into the first formally legislated Militia formation. Able-bodied men, ages 16 to 60, were ordered to muster on the village green at a specified day and time for marksmanship and regimental marching practice. The term of service was short, and upon completion, the men returned to their roles as ordinary citizens.

Specifically, the legislation from the Records of the Colony of The Massachusetts Bay in New England read thus:

> 315 It is ordered, that all military men in this iurisdiction shalbee ranked into three regiments, viz, Boston, Roxberry, Dorchester, Weimoth, Hingham, to bee one regiment, whereof John Winthrope, Senior, Esquir, shalbee colonell, & Tho : Dudley, Esquir, leiftenent colonell;

---

[6] David V. Stivison, ed. *Magna Carta in America* (Baltimore: Gateway Press, 1993), 17.
[7] Doubler, *Civilian in Peace, Soldier in War*, 9.

Charlestowne, Newetowne, Watertowne, Concord, & Deddam to bee another regiment wherof John Haynes, Esqr, shalbee colonell, & Roge Herlakenden, Esqr, leiftenant colonell;

Saugust, Salem, Ipswich, & Neweberry to bee another regiment, whereof John Endecot, Esqr, shalbee colonell, & John Winthrope, Junior, leiftenant colonell;

& the Governor for the time being shalbee cheife generall./

And each severall regiment shall make choyce of such men as they shall think most fit & safe for the servise & trust of those places of colonel & leiftenant colonell, & psent them by their deputies to the next session of this Court; & for the captaines & leiftenants to the severall companies the severall townes shall make shoice of some principall man, or two, or three, in each towne, & psent them to the counsell, who shall appoint one of them to the said office in each company./

And each regiment shall have one muster master, who shall have yearly maintenance out of the treasury, viz, to bee paid quarterly to evry of them. The said three mustermasters for the psent shalbee Captaine Traske for the east regiment, Capt Vnderhill for the south regiment, and Capt Patrick for the north regiment. The power & imployment of all the said comaunders & mustermasters shall, fro time to time, bee ordered by the Governor & counsell, or by the counsell of warr, when any shalbee established./ [8]

The Colony's recognition of the duty to protect the village did not spring forth like Athena from Zeus's forehead, fully armed and ready for war.[9] It had deep roots in the Enlightenment thinking of Western Europe that also blossomed in the seventeenth century. The philosophy of Immanuel Kant (1724-1804), for example, wended its way from Germany to the New World with the educators of the time who founded Harvard in Massachusetts and Yale in Connecticut, among other institutions of higher learning. While the individual citizens on the commons in Salem, Massachusetts in 1636 might not have been able to quote the criteria for Kant's Categorical Imperative, the Categorical Imperative

---

[8] Shurtleff, *Records of the Governor and Company of the Massachusetts Bay of New England*, Vol. I, 1628-1641, 186-187.
[9] Edith Hamilton, *Mythology* (Boston: Little, Brown, & Company, 1942), 29. Greek mythology has it that Zeus' daughter Athena – Goddess of War and Wisdom – sprang from her father's forehead as an adult, fully clothed in armor and well-armed.

itself is timeless and the descendants of those citizens would be familiar with Enlightenment concepts. Additionally, the hardships of living in a wild new land and confronting the indigenous population that was not always friendly, led to a more practical need for group protection.

The concept of a village and then state militia became the norm throughout the original thirteen colonies. A native of the British colony of Virginia, then George Washington (1732-1749), served as a Major in the Virginia militia and in the French and Indian War of 1753. The French, in northern territories that later would become eastern Canada (Ontario and Quebec, to be specific), allied with Indian raiders to do battle with Vermont[10] and the neighboring colonies. The War spread from New England as far south as Pennsylvania before reaching its conclusion. With regards to the difference, in Washington's view, between the British regular soldiers and his militiamen from the colonies he wrote after Braddock's Defeat at the Monongahela River in Pennsylvania,

> Our numbers consisted of about thirteen hundred well armed men, chiefly Regulars[11], who were immediately struck with such an inconceivable panick [sic], that nothing byt [sic] confusion and disobedience of orders prevailed among them....The Virginia companies behaved like men and died like soldiers...[12]

As was typical, when his service ended in 1758, Colonel Washington resigned his commission in the Virginia Militia and returned to his family and farm. Not until 1775, did the Second Continental Congress in Philadelphia agree to establish a Continental Army. But, when they did and the Army became necessary in the pursuit of Independence, the Continental Congress looked to Colonel (ret.) George Washington to be its first Commander in Chief.

Having been educated at the young age of seventeen at the College of William and Mary, General Washington would certainly have been familiar with the ideas swirling around and through the Enlightenment. By 1776, he found himself embroiled in the Revolutionary War and in command of a Continental Army. Alongside this "regular" army fought the Militias of which he had so recently been a member. Eugene Clements and F. Edward Wright put together an excellent monograph on the history of one of the colonial militias in particular. By focusing on the state of Maryland, Clements and Wright in *The*

---

[10] Vermont: so close to the French Canadian border that its very name is a French compound of vert and mont for "Green Mountain".

[11] "Regulars" referred to the British troops.

[12] W.W. Abbot, ed., *The Papers of George Washington: Colonial Series volume 1, 1748 - August 1755* (Charlottesville and London: University Press of Virginia, 1983), 118-9.

Maryland Militia in the Revolutionary War, assist genealogists in their pursuit of tracking down relatives who served.[13] Their study of the Maryland militia is a wonderful disarticulation of the events of the war as well as the parallel service performed by the Continental Army and its sister militias. Overall, Clements and Wright recount the exploits of a grassroots, almost ad-hoc group of militias that grew out of the original "trayned band" concept. Yet, it becomes quite clear that these men are well familiar with their local surroundings and are able to incorporate their limited muster training with intimate knowledge of the rivers, creeks, and forests of the Maryland coastlines from Patuxent River to Annapolis, to Baltimore and all along the Eastern Shore. Remarkably, Maryland militias even took part in the Battle of Brooklyn, 1776. Giving example after example, Clements and Wright demonstrate the clever use the locals are put to – without ever missing an opportunity to also note the shenanigans they get into. Since the bulk of the book is designed to assist genealogists, the limited space for narrative illustrates the significance of the local citizenry acting as independent units in the defense of their communities. One must note that – while the Kantian ideals of the Categorical Imperative might have been wafting through the minds of the citizens, at an individual level, they were by no means uniform. Desertion, drunkenness, illness (feigned or otherwise) were rampant in the early militias. Nevertheless, by the eighteenth century, the concept of the citizen-soldier in a state militia was well established. Along with the militias that provide fundamental structure, a standing army (the Continental Army) is also created for professional soldiers in 1775.

Following victory in the Revolutionary War, the colonies struggled to form a union and yet finalized the Constitution and ratified it in 1789. Western Europeans, with influential academics still deep in the Enlightenment, watched the fledgling experiment in "government of the people, by the people, and for the people" with a mix of horror and envy. In the New World, time wore on and more territory added to the original thirteen. By 1803, Thomas Jefferson was president and the Louisiana Purchase added almost a full third of the land of what the United States would become.

[W]hen we speak of the common soldier of the American Revolution…for Virginians, we are talking about … farmers who were

---

[13] Eugene S. Clements and F. Edward Wright, *The Maryland Militia in the Revolutionary War* (Westminster: Heritage Books, 2006), in general.

destined to make several moves westward....[If] they wanted something better, the frontier was their best hope of attaining it.[14]

Thus inspired, the American mind began to look West for wealth, adventure, fertile land to farm, and freedom not unlike the drive that brought their forebears across the ocean over one hundred years before. That drive and mission was soon to be known as "Manifest Destiny." Philosophically, America also started to develop its own personality – Henry David Thoreau (1817-1862) and Ralph Waldo Emerson (1803-1882) would create a school of thought called the Transcendentalists who believed above all in the superiority of nature, in self-reliance, and in natural rights. William James, an admirer of Emerson's, would go on to create the well-known American philosophy of Pragmatism.

While these philosophical theories spread throughout the young United States, the emphasis on individual rights led to a deep distrust of a standing Federal armed force. Beginning as far back as the Revolutionary War, the distrust of a standing, powerful army was rooted in the fear of the original British Army used to enforce the "unreasonable" burdens of the English monarchy. Although manifested in the republican form of government devised by the early colonial leaders, the threat of perceived oppression by a large, career army was entrenched throughout the ordinary citizenry as well. While discussing the basic authority in the Constitution for the establishment of "armies", Marion and Hoffman note, "The Founders chose their words carefully....It reflected the traditional fear of standing armies, brought from Europe and reinforce by the colonial experience".[15] The Continental Army (renamed the Army of the United States in 1784) maintained fewer numbers while the individual state militias continued to exist unabated. On a return victory tour in 1825, the Marquis de Lafayette visited the United States and famously reviewed the New York Militia, 2d Battalion, 11th New York Artillery.

---

[14] Stanley J. Underdal, Maj., ed. *Military History of the American Revolution: Proceedings of the 6th Military History Symposium United States Air Force Academy, 10-11 October 1974* (Washington D.C.: Office of Air Force History USAF and United States Air Force Academy, 1976), 161.
[15] Forrest L. Marion and Jon T. Hoffman, *Forging a Total Force* (Washington, D. C.: Historical Office, Office of the Secretary of Defense, 2018), 3.

Figure 2.1: "Lafayette and the National Guard", by Ken Riley.

The Marquis de Lafayette inspects the 2nd Battalion, 11th New York Artillery in 1825 during his visit to the United States between 1824 and 1825. (Heritage Collection)

The New York leadership was so grateful for the Marquis' service during the Revolution that they honored him by naming themselves the Guard Nationale, after Lafayette's command in the French Army. In an elegantly penned letter from Lt. Col. Edmunds to Captain John Forbes, Edmunds writes,

Dear Sir, La Fayette is expected to visit this City in the course of next week and the uniform Companies of the 47th Rgt. Will be called out on the occasion. We should be very happy to be honored with your Company in the [procession] on the occasion. The precise time of his visit is not yet known. When it is, I will communicate the same to you....Truly yours, M. W. Edmonds, Lt. Col, 47th Infantry, Commanding Infy [illegible]....[16]

---

[16] Lt. Col. Edmonds to Capt. John Forbes, Forbes Letters, National Guard Memorial Museum, Library, and Archives, Washington, D.C.

Figure 2.2: Lt. Col. Edmonds to Capt. John Forbes, 1824.

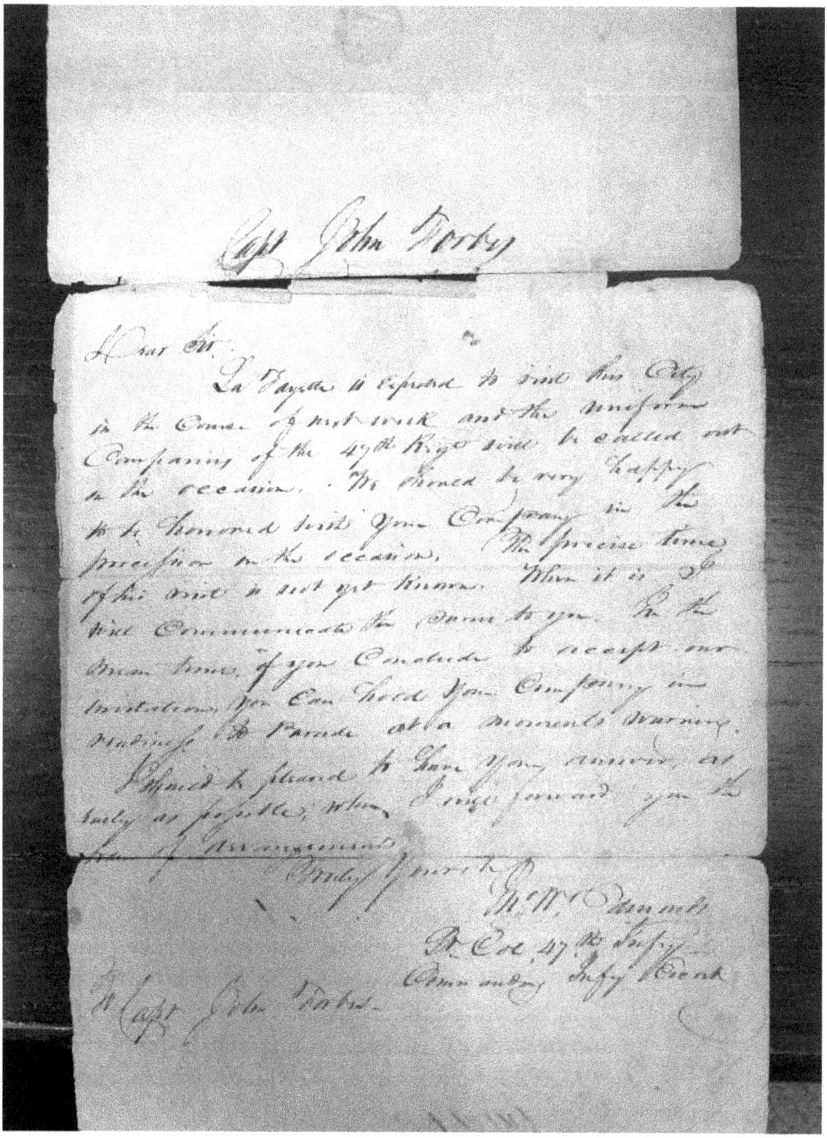

Captain John Forbes is instructed to muster for the visit of the Marquis de Lafayette in 1824. (National Guard Educational Foundation Collection)

By way of reply to the pomp and circumstance put on for the visit of such a great hero, the General replied to his well-wishers, "[M]ay all the nations who resort to this flourishing place, reflect on the blessings of a free constitution, and the dignity of a self-governed people".[17] Anecdotally, William Swinton (1833-1892) wrote in 1870,

> [O]n the evening of the 25th of August, 1824, the officers of the four companies of the Infantry Battalion of the old Eleventh Regiment [NY], at a meeting held at the Shakespeare Tavern, adopted a resolution to the effect that said battalion "be hereafter known and distinguished by the name of National Guards." … On this occasion reference was made, by someone present, to La Fayette's connection with the Paris National Guard, when immediately Major John D. Wilson asked why "National Guards" would not be a good name for the proposed corps? This electric utterance at once crystallized their desires in a fixed purpose…[and] a few days later … the resolution to adopt the designation of "National Guards" was enthusiastically passed.[18]

Interestingly, William Swinton emigrated from Scotland to the U.S. in 1843 and studied at Amherst. He was a New York teacher who collaborated with Walt Whitman and was a war correspondent for the New York Times during the American Civil War.[19] By 1903, the name "National Guard" was formally adopted by all the states in reference to their growing militias.[20]

As the United States began to grow comfortable in its own safety and security, the nation's leadership recognized troubles brewing beyond its own growing borders, particularly in the south and west along the Mexican border. In 1846, the Mexican-American War broke out and was almost entirely manned over land by National Guardsmen. Famous soldiers in this war included future presidents Zachary Taylor, James K. Polk, and Franklin Pierce, and future Civil War generals Winfield Scott, and John C. Fremont. Although a far cry from the lofty Enlightenment teaching halls of Boston, New Haven, and Williamsburg, the citizen-soldiers of the day personified the Enlightenment sentiment of serving one's country and home territory when confronted with an armed enemy. They were emboldened by self-reliance and individualism inspired by living on the new, rugged continent. Manifest Destiny, a name coined by John

---

[17] The Marquis de Lafayette, accompanied by his son George Washington Lafayette, Author unknown, *The Independent Inquirer and Commercial Advertiser*, (Providence), August 26, 1824.

[18] William Swinton, *History of the Seventh Regiment, National Guard* (New York: Bields, Osgood, & Co., 1870), 2-3.

[19] "The Vault at Pfaff's, An Archive of Art and Literature by the Bohemians of Antebellum New York," The Vault at Pfaff's, accessed July 15, 2018, https://pfaffs.web.lehigh.edu/node/54195.

[20] Codified in the U.S. Congress' "Dick Act" of 1903 (about which we will learn more later).

L. O'Sullivan in 1839, became the rallying cry as citizen-soldiers pushed West, confronting resistance as they met it.[21] In an 1856 review of Alexander Humboldt's, *The Island of Cuba*, the editor of the United States Democratic Review, Spencer W. Cone wrote, "a general perusal of this work... will tend to hasten the chariot-wheels of the *destiny* which promises to absorb the whole Northern continent, ... in one confederated bond of liberty".[22]

By the 1860s, the country disintegrated over the regional disagreements as to the legality of the institution of slavery and the state militias returned to their respective "corners" – fighting state against state, militia against militia. The Kantian ideal of voluntary service in defense of one's state and institutions was in full force as the militias waged a brutal war against each other. Militias served in the Civil War side-by-side with the small Federal Army but both were vastly outnumbered by Federal Volunteer Forces that had built up after the Punitive War with Mexico in 1846. By 1865, the South succumbed to its various weaknesses and the Union rose victorious. The structure of the National Guard was to undergo a dramatic reorganization and purpose. With an understanding of the importance of Washington D.C. as the headquarters of the newly re-united states, the leadership of the National Guard recognized the need to consolidate their voices. Although originally two separate organizations, the National Guard Association of the United States (NGAUS)[23] emerged as a single voice in 1878. Also in 1878, the Federal Government passed the law of *Posse Comitatus* that stemmed from the colonial era of British soldiers entering homes without leave. The law simply stated that no Federal soldier may enforce local laws within a sovereign state. Therefore, a National Guardsman on state duty could enforce a Federal law and a local law but a federal soldier had no authority over local regulations. Having been used extensively in Civil War Reconstruction, the Regular full-time Army grew to be commonly used for strike breaking along with the citizen-soldiers. To arrest this development, the *Posse Comitatus* Act of 1878 required the federal soldiers only to act under direct orders from the President of the United States. Thereby, Governors maintained authority over their respective National Guard forces, while the Federal troops were no longer available to quell domestic civil disorder.[24] To this day, that law remains largely unchanged. By the 1890s, the National Guard

---

[21] Spencer W. Cone, ed., *The United States Democratic Review*, Jan-Jun (New York: Lloyd & Company, 1839) 426-430, accessed July 19, 2018, https://babel.hathitrust.org/cgi/pt?id=mdp.39015035929606;view=1up;seq=426.

[22] Ibid., 594.

[23] NGAUS is inexplicably pronounced GNAW-gus.

[24] That is not to say the National Guard troops could not be "Federalized" which will become used during the civil disorder of the 1960s. Once Federalized, the National Guard falls under the President's command.

was pulled in a tug of war between the civil disorder of the massive coal and rail strikes as well as the international questions posed by the Philippines Insurrection and the Spanish-American War of 1898. To combat the problems posed by sending National Guardsmen beyond the US borders, and in support of the relatively small standing Army, National Guardsmen were permitted to be federalized on individual bases and entire regiments were allowed to be federalized as volunteer units.[25]

Following the Spanish-American War, the narrative arguably led to the most significant turning point in the history of the National Guard, the passage of the The Militia Act of 1903 or "The Dick Act." The Dick Act was named for Major General Charles W. F. Dick (1858-1945) of the Ohio National Guard. An incomparable leader of his time, Dick had been in the Spanish American War as a young officer in the Guard, thrived there and reached the rank of Major General, commanding the entire Ohio Army. In 1902, he became the President of NGAUS and served in that capacity until 1909. He ran for the House of Representatives, won in 1898, and then served as the Ohio Senator in 1904.[26] Significantly, he was also a majority shareholder in the Goodyear Rubber and Tire Company, which was taking full advantage of a South American rubber glut and a craving for tires to outfit new motorized vehicles. The largest cosmetic change brought about by the passage of the Dick Act was to formalize the name, National Guard. The most organic change, though, came in funding, equipping, and training. The National Guard was to finally and formally mirror the active duty in all aspects of readiness. The soldiers in the local militias would wear the same uniforms, use the same equipment, train with adherence to the same regulations, and – critically – be paid the same as their full-time counterparts.[27] "It is hard to overstate the significance of the Dick Act for the National Guard. The practices of the volunteer militia as a self-supporting and largely independent entity gave way to a new military force with significant federal funding and subject to the administrative controls of the War Department".[28] Thus armed, the National Guard was poised to take on the earth-shattering ghastly brutality of World War One.

---

[25] "For example, the 1st Regiment, New York National Guard, was redesignated the 1st Regiment, Infantry, New York Volunteers". Marion and Hoffman, *Forging a Total Force*, 11.
[26] It is unclear how he was able to be President of NGAUS (a lobbying organization) and a Congressman steering the Dick Act and its amendment in 1908 through the governmental system concurrently. Today, a lobbyist may not serve on any Federal status.
[27] The Dick Act is the seed from which the 1973 Total Force Policy would grow into today's formidable Post-9/11 Era fighting force.
[28] Doubler, *Civilian in Peace, Soldier in War*, 144.

Although the First World War started in Europe in August 1914, the United States did not enter the War until April 1917. Prior to the U.S. entry, however, President Wilson's and Congressional attention was focused on a second conflict with Mexico that involved the National Guard. It is important to understand that in 1912, U.S. Attorney General George W. Wickersham read the Constitution with a narrowly tailored interpretation to hold that the National Guard could not be used by the President of the United States for any duty so long as they remained National Guardsmen in state service. Meanwhile, acting on the provisions of the 1903 Dick Act, NGAUS and the National Guard had begun a push for Universal Mandatory Training (UMT) that would get the militias trained to the same level of readiness as the regular Army. Although UMT would never really be enacted, the initial conflict posed by the Wickersham decision and the attempts being made by the Guard to become more and more like the standing Army gave a great shock to the system. Necessity willed out when, in March of 1916, Mexico's incursions into American territory demanded a response and the National Guard was ready. While Federal troops crossed over into Mexico, the border-states mustered their militias to protect themselves from attack. Practically concurrently, the Congress passed the Militia Act of 1916 that permitted the President to Federalize the National Guard and use them across international borders.

When the call came to enter World War One in April of 1917, the National Guard was ready to mobilize. Between the end of the Civil War in 1865 and entry into World War One in 1917, the National Guard had been through an almost complete transformation. What started as a depleted and demoralized local citizen-soldier force grew into formal Infantry Divisions to rival even the most organized active duty Federal Army Division. By 1917, 18 Divisions of National Guardsmen were sent to the European theatre. These divisions included representatives from every state but also, very significantly, included "negro soldiers". African American National Guardsmen were sent over with one major restriction – their "segregation requirements" were too onerous for them to fight with white Americans. The separate but equal doctrine used in the United States meant that the Army Leadership ordered that these soldiers required separate messing facilities as well as separate latrines, sleeping quarters, as well as medical and support staff. So, as a compromise, two divisions fought with the French, who did not require racially segregated units. The African American guardsmen worked primarily as stevedores and labor battalions. Many soldiers found themselves squarely on the front lines of the combat. Originally awarded the Croix de Guerre, several African American guardsmen would find posthumous recognition with Medals of Honor in the late twentieth and early twenty-first centuries.

During the early twentieth century, the origins of military aviation began with a small band of civilians in New York who had an interest in ballooning. In 1908, they dubbed themselves the 1st Company, Signal Corps, New York National Guard. Although it is not clear whether they actually got airborne, they represent the beginnings of what would become, by the end of World War Two, the Air National Guard of the United States. As the Army Guard determined to fashion itself in the image of the standing, regular Army, the beginning of the Air National Guard grew out of the Army Guard. They would remain with the Army as Observation Squadrons relegated to supporting Army maneuvers from the sky. Captain Charles A. Lindbergh of the Missouri National Guard was easily the most famous member of an observation squadron. In true citizen-soldier fashion, he stated later, "[P]ilots 'joined the Guard for two reasons that still hold up: first, the opportunity it offered to keep in flying training, and second, they considered it a patriotic duty to keep fit for immediate service in the case of a wartime emergency'".[29] From a philosophical perspective, Lindbergh summed up the concept of the citizen-soldier from an aviator's standpoint – stay fit and ready in case of an emergency but, otherwise, remain in a civilian capacity. Dr. Charles J. Gross, the author of *Air National Guard at 60: A History* goes on to say, "in the pre-World War II period, Guard aviators also honored the citizen-soldier tradition by assisting civil authorities in domestic emergencies, most notably during the devastating Mississippi River flood of April and May 1927".[30] Holding a relatively small Army mission, the aviation support did not catch many eyes of the military or civilian leadership until after World War Two. However, by 1946, as the Air Force branched off the regular Army, the 120th Observation Squadron of Colorado became the first federally recognized Air National Guard squadron. As the Air Force became a separate branch of service, the Air National Guard found itself comprised of fifty-eight thousand men and recognition of its own.

If philosophy may be viewed as a bellwether to alert people of broad and deep changes in the fabric of their culture, philosophers certainly reacted accordingly to the horrors of World War One. The National Guard's role in the United States reflected the same disillusionment with established order. In the particular case of the United States and its impression on the National Guard, restrictions in funding diminished the role of the Citizen-soldier in service. The philosophy of the Enlightenment and the unchanging, reliable nature of Reason was shaken to its core. The United States began to pull in on itself and turn away from the European troubles following the ravages of the World War.

---

[29] Gross, Charles J. and Susan Rosenfeld, *Air National Guard at 60: A History* (Washington, D.C.: Department of the Air Force, 2007), 5-6.
[30] Ibid.

The Pre-War Progressive Era in America had proven to the military leaders like Pershing and Dick that the future was bright and golden. War was fought on a relatively close shore and in the interest of local defense, protection, and advantage. The Kantian ideals of universality of goals, of a sense of fairness, and a clear purpose in a voluntary force in which man is not used as a means to an end but used with his own intellectual authority was dashed by the experiences of World War One. An understanding of protecting your own shores was not even relevant – the war was fought on foreign soil for arguably foreign purposes. Although the Philippines Insurrection and the Spanish-American Wars had been fought on foreign shores, they were limited in scope and duration. In World War One, any sense of fairness was lost in the trenches and succumbed to rampant indiscriminate use of mustard gas and other agents. As for the idea of not using a man as a means to an end? Well, after that experience, who would ever return of their own volition to such hell? The philosophy of the day began to waiver in its certainty – it began to question Reason in the face of the utterly unreasonable. And, unsurprisingly, so did the role of the National Guard. With the advent of World War One, we see a great shift in philosophy to the Post-Modern despair of systematic mass annihilation. The shift grew exponentially darker with the end of World War Two in which seventeen National Guard Divisions partook – two that liberate the concentration camp at Dachau and two that took direct part in the dropping of the bombs in Hiroshima and Nagasaki. As philosophy descended into what can be called the despair and iconoclasm of Post-Modernism, so did the prefect application of the Kantian ideal to the Citizen-soldier in the United States.

In order to adjust to this new, bleaker world than the one of the Gilded Age, the National Guard began to review its role in the American military landscape. The standing Army, although shell-shocked and somewhat demoralized, had grown in stature and numbers. This rapid growth further ballooned because of the devastating effects of the Great Depression that hit the country and the world hard on October 29th, 1929. Within months, the number of homeless, destitute, desperately unemployed men choked the cities and thronged the farmland of the United States. The National Guard rose to the occasion by employing more and more civilians as Guardsmen. The Guard began opening the doors of their Armories to provide shelter for the homeless and soup kitchens for the hungry. By 1933, the Federal government realized the need to include the National Guard in its augmented standing army and

> [s]ince 1933, the National Guard became the "National Guard of the United States" when in federal service; at other times, it is the National

Guard of the particular state. This dual status must be remembered in any consideration of the Guard's function or operations.[31]

When President Franklin Delano Roosevelt began the Works Progress Administration (WPA) in May of 1935, newly employed civilians were set to work building new Armories to provide comfort to even more desperate citizens. For the most part, the citizens of the United States recognized the universal duty to serve, the fairness of helping each other in equal measures, and that the provision of food and shelter to the desperate while working toward a common goal was hardly the use of men as a means to an end.

Through such opportunities and community service, the National Guard ranks swelled. The National Guard leadership, in an effort to remain true to its tradition as citizen-soldiers, put forth a full-throated argument for Universal Military Training (UMT). The concept was based in the part-time nature of the Guard and recommended that Guardsmen continue to commit to the weekend duty and training periods that had been laid out in the Dick Act of 1903. The major change, however, was that that the entire male population between 16 and 60 years of age in the United States serve a mandatory period of service in the Guard. The leadership argued that, if we have a well-trained part-time force that was mandatory and covered the entire population of eligible men, then the National Guard could support the regular Army at a moment's notice and fully-fledged. Although UMT was never implemented, the argument was a forceful and seductive one. It remained on the table through the Second World War and into the 1950s. UMT was only derailed by the civil disorder of the 1960s and the Vietnam War protests – both of which caused unanticipated domestic turmoil for the National Guard.

In 1948, NGAUS lobbied successfully to obtain for all National Guardsmen pensions dating from individual service in 1916 (later amended to 1903.) Not only did this sort of financial benefit appeal to members of the Guard, it aided in recruitment and the number of members in the Guard swelled between World War Two and the Korean War. By the 1960s in the United States, the National Guard relived its tug of war between international missions and domestic civil disorder. Authorized and emboldened by the still current *Posse Comitatus* Act of 1878 and the National Defense Acts from 1916 forward, President Lyndon B. Johnson was ready, willing, and able to federalize the National Guard to enforce Federal laws domestically. What he was not willing

---

[31] National Association of Attorneys General, Committee on the Office of Attorney General, *Legal Issues Concerning the Role of the National Guard in Civil Disorders: Staff Report to the Special Committee on Legal Services to Military Forces* (Washington D.C.: General Printing Office, 1973), 9.

to do, however, was commit National Guardsmen to international wars – like the ones simmering in East Asia. Since the 1950s, the Soviet Union and China, in their attempts to influence or install puppet states in other countries, had represented threats of the spread of Communism. The threat frightened the United States both at home and abroad, however rationally or irrationally. Within the United States, the McCarthy Hearings became emblematic of the "Red Scare". Internationally, Johnson perpetuated the concept led by Harry Truman before him of the Domino Theory and Containment. Essentially, these theories state that if one country fell to Communist rule under the influence of the USSR or China, then more were to follow. In order to prevent such a catastrophe, American troops or "advisors" were necessary in country to contain the spread. Johnson knew that, by sending ordinary citizens over to Asia who could be missed, he would show his hand and create social upheaval. So, with intent, Johnson decided to begin with advisors and, when combat broke out, to send the full-time force but leave the National Guard at home. Service in the National Guard became an opportunity to avoid the draft for an unpopular war through deferment rather than a way to serve your country and community. The Kantian Categorical Imperative was virtually unrecognizable as any influence over military service during this period of National Guard history with terrible results. The citizen-soldier model failed to be enacted universally (as seen by the complicated deferment issues), the nation rebelled in the face of "unfair" (or unequal) drafting of citizens to become soldiers, and the resulting population of soldiers actually sent to combat represented the government's use of men as a means to an end (use those who could not avoid the service as combat soldiers in the line of fire rather than those who could avoid the draft.)

On the other hand, the mission of the National Guard during the domestic strife of the 1960s adhered to the Categorical Imperative structure. The country was faced with a racial divide along the lines of Dr. Martin Luther King, Jr.'s non-violence and the militant factions as well as increased anti-war sentiment across the college campuses. As described in the previous paragraph, most of the active-duty U.S. military was across the world, fighting the controversial conflict in East Asia, leaving the National Guard stateside to assist the local constabulary. Having never been altered, the law of *Posse Comitatus* from 1878 was still good law – no Federal military member could enforce local laws. In addition, having been tweaked over the years, the original National Defense Act of 1916 allowed for the federalization of National Guardsmen. Combining these two concepts left the Federal government free to federalize the National Guard in support of the enforcement of Federal Laws. Therefore, when the Civil Rights Act of 1964 passed and was signed in to law, the National Guard was available to enforce its application. Between 1965 and 1968, the National Guard received additional riot control training and prepared for the riots that broke out after

Dr. King's assassination in April of that year. It is important to note that Guardsmen were on both Federal and state orders during these dark days. The most famous National Guard incident during these years was the riot control at Kent State University in May of 1970. After the secret invasion of Cambodia authorized by President Richard M. Nixon became public, the campus erupted into vicious riots. On May 4th, armed with tear gas and bayonets, 115 troops tried to suppress the rioters. After running out of tear gas and under a renewed assault by the students armed with rocks, some thirty Guardsmen opened fire. Four students were killed and nine injured. Six days later, a bomb blasted through the glass walls of the NGAUS headquarters on Massachusetts Ave., NW, Washington, D.C.

Based on these cultural changes in the United States from 1948 and 1970, "nearly every … aspect of the National Guard service changed…[but t]he American people continued to rely on Guardsmen for national defense and for assistance during natural disasters and domestic disturbances".[32] In 1970, Secretary of Defense Melvin Laird and Theodore C. Marrs, an Air National Guardsman from Alabama, articulated the "total force concept". Based on Marrs' concept, and with a nod to Congressman Charles' Dick's Act of 1903, the American military would now increase reliance on the Guard and the Reserve as a cornerstone of the United States' defense policy. With full intent, Laird knew that the inclusion of the Guard would help win the flagging support of the American people by accounting for the interests of state and local constituencies. The Total Force concept intended to recognize the need for a national vested interest for communities and their contribution to the defense of the nation. In other words, an aspect of the Total Force Policy meant to bring the nation's attention to community-level service in the military defense of the interests of the country as a whole. Thereby, in reverse, the local communities could become more invested in contributing to the national defense. In a 1973 speech to the TRADOC/FORSCOM Chaplain Training Conference, in Kansas City, MO, General Creighton Abrams made the famous statement, "If the unfortunate circumstance should occur that…we would have to use the Army again, then we will use the active, the National Guard, and the reserve together….If an army is going to be worth anything to its country in the hour of need, it has got to do it from the heart".[33] This statement brings up the spectre of the American heart – a repeated but ill-defined American concept.

---

[32] Doubler, *Civilian in Peace, Soldier in War*, 266-7.
[33] "The Way of the Soldier: Remembering General Creighton Abrams," Foreign Policy Research Institute, accessed April 2, 2019, https://www.fpri.org/article/2013/05/the-way-of-the-soldier-remembering-general-creighton-abrams/

In the case of the "heart of America" for General Abrams, I believe he referred directly to that very Kantian Categorical Imperative inherited from the Enlightenment. General Abrams, I believe, understood that the citizen-soldier represented the moral duty to serve as a universal, fair, and voluntary sacrifice to the defense of our right to life, liberty, and the pursuit of happiness. For General Creighton Abrams, the citizen-soldier represented a universal, moral duty of citizens.[34] What was dubbed "The Abrams Doctrine" became formal policy in 1973 with the help of Laird, Marrs, and the new Secretary of Defense, Arthur M. Schlesinger.

In order to reinvigorate a demoralized United States Army, General Creighton presided over a structural change known as the Roundout Brigades. The National Guard would supply an entire brigade to each Army Division in order to round them out to full strength. Starting in Hawaii in 1973 and a success by all accounts, Roundout continued and, through the program, brought the citizen-soldier concept into accord with the full-time regular Army. The development of the Air National Guard during this period, as a part of the Air Force, the youngest branch of the full-time force, paralleled development of the Army National Guard. This development coalesced in the "Air Land Battle" doctrine. Because the Air National Guard paralleled the development of the Air Force, assets were used in concert and "the attack of enemy forces in depth [would be synchronized with] the maximum combat power from all the military services into a coordinated, joint effort".[35] This program became reality when, in 1990, Saddam Hussein of Iraq invaded the sovereign nation of Kuwait. On August 2, 1990, U.S. active duty armed forces were placed on alert as Hussein's offensive forces rolled into Kuwait. Having learned the rough lessons of Vietnam, President George H. W. Bush began immediately activating the National Guard and the Reserves. While the initial call-up was limited mainly to command Arabic speakers, by the end of the war voluntary service resulted in over 62.400 Guardsmen in almost 400 units deployed to the Persian Gulf. Interestingly, the Roundout brigades remained in the US. The primary reason is one that still plagues the National Guard today – the missions require immediate response and the nature of the National Guard is more readily used in a delayed deployment. In fact, the CENTCOM heavy force request came a full ten days before President Bush authorized Guard callup.[36] A continuing issue in the ongoing debate for funding both the active duty and the National Guard, the existence of Roundout Brigades ensure the debate will continue for the foreseeable future. The argument of the adherence to the Categorical

---

[34] Ibid.
[35] Doubler, *Civilian in Peace, Soldier in War*, 288.
[36] Ibid., 312-333.

Imperative and its effect on the concept of the citizen-soldier does not obviate the use of the active duty entirely. Simply making the argument that the active-duty is better trained and equipped to handle short-notice contingencies does not mean that they should not be backed-up, relieved, and even shored up by National Guardsmen. Notice that the argument here is not a Utilitarian one. Although the National Guard is well suited as a reserve force for the Active Duty, that is a consequence-based concept. There is a normative argument to be made, as well. The National Guard has proven that it is the best force to handle emergency domestic contingencies. Federal service certainly has a moral aspect of its own. But it is the National Guard citizen-soldier who serves under the moral authority of the Kantian Categorical Imperative we trace back to our Enlightenment roots. He or she is the ordinary citizen who serves to protect the community in which they hold life, liberty, and the pursuit of property most dear. The actual timeline of Operation Desert Shield/Storm (ODS/S) can be described as the Powell Doctrine, named for General Colin Powell to establish clear goals, prepare thoroughly for the entire mission, and then attack. Then, once the mission is accomplished, withdraw forces and then withdraw the preparedness equipment. Operation Desert Shield consisted of the preparation and the redeployment. In the middle of the timeline, Operation Desert Storm consisted of the actual period of combat. By the beginning of Storm, January 17, 1991, the National Guard troops were fully up to speed and fought shoulder-to-shoulder with their active-duty partners. The last National Guard troops to leave theatre headed home by July 23rd, 1991. Thus marked the end of the first rendering of the Total Force Policy in action.

The 1990s ushered in a new role for the National Guard on the global front. Only two years before, the Berlin Wall had come down – marking the end of the Cold War and the United States responded by taking a more relaxed posture as the world's police force. With the success of ODS/S, the US was able to begin a dramatic downsizing in its deployed forces and those on duty within the Continental United States. President George H. W. Bush referred to the now vastly more peaceful international situation as "The New World Order". Containment was no longer the primary mission of the US and we could now focus on a "bottom-up review (BUR)" run by the new head of the Joint Chiefs of Staff, General Colin Powell. Suddenly, all felt, the active duty could draw down, the US would benefit from the "peace dividend" and the National Guard could reap the benefits. A cheaper force overall, the National Guard could serve in the less demanding capacity than the active duty – and the U.S. could heave a collective sigh.

The role of the Guard shifted from an offensive back up for the active duty Army and Air Force and became peacekeepers, involved in the upheaval in Eastern Europe marked by the disintegration of the former Soviet Union

(USSR). After service during strife in Somalia and Ethiopia, the National Guard was well-prepared for its mission in the Balkans in 1995. In 1991, Slovenia and Croatia had declared independence from Yugoslavia. In a couple of months, Bosnia-Herzegovina and Macedonia followed suit. In Serbia, President Slobodan Milosevic used military force to hold the area together. Between Bosnia and Croatia, long-simmering ethnic hatreds boiled into a froth. Tragically, the Serbians resorted to ethnic cleansing as a means of control. President William J. Clinton brought the nations together to negotiate an end to the conflict, and the Dayton Peace Accords of November 1995 were finally signed in December 1995 in Paris. The Accords included American peacekeeping forces and the National Guard was ready, willing, and able to meet the demand. Ultimately, over 8,000 National Guardsmen served in the Balkan peacekeeping forces through 1998.

During the early 1990s, the domestic mission of the National Guard continued unabated. Civil rights continued to be an issue and the riots caused by the videotaped evidence surrounding the police beating of motorist Rodney King during a traffic stop resulted in an uprising in Los Angeles. The National Guard responded to hurricanes, floods, and other natural disasters as well as those that were man-made. Domestic Terrorism was on the rise – as evidenced by the Oklahoma City bombing of the Alfred P. Murrah Building in 1995 and the Waco, TX standoff with religious zealots in 1993. In Oklahoma City, 731 Guardsmen immediately answered the call to duty; 624 soldiers and 107 airmen.[37] In Waco, Texas, rather than being on the front line, the National Guard of Texas and Alabama provided support to a primarily Bureau of Alcohol, Tobacco, and Firearms (ATF) mission. Also in 1993, Islamic fundamentalists blew up the underground basement parking lot of the World Trade Center – a terrorist act that brought the New York National Guard into full force and foreshadowed the ghastly events of September 11, 2001.

On that cool, clear day in 2001, the National Guard of the United States was called upon to do something it had never done before – defend the nation from a terrorist attack while also tending to its domestic mission of providing disaster relief within the nation's own borders. While the New York National Guard raced to Manhattan in an immediate response to the airplane crashes at the World Trade Center, the District of Columbia National Guard raced to the Pentagon in response to the airplane crash there. Soon after, the Pennsylvania National Guard was en route to Shanksville, Pennsylvania to do the same. For all three emergency responses, the National Guard had to react as a disaster

---

[37] "Guardmembers remember Oklahoma City bombing," Army.mil, accessed July 6, 2018, https://www.army.mil/article/37587/guardmembers_remember_oklahoma_city_bombing

preparedness force as well. When the crippled towers in Manhattan finally fell, the damage to Lower Manhattan was catastrophic. The Pentagon and surrounding areas burned for hours; likewise the fields of Pennsylvania. By the time the Guard had the three situations under control locally, the entire National Guard of the United States was reacting to the national disaster as a whole – continental airspace was cleared, transportation ground to a halt, and practically all communication was smothered by news of the attacks. The country reeled from the horror for weeks before the National Guard was mobilized and deployed overseas with the Federal Army in the attack on Afghanistan called Operation Enduring Freedom (OEF).

OEF began on October 7, 2001, and began what would be called the Global War on Terror (GWOT.)[38] The primary change in the National Guard and the concept of the citizen-soldier was the transition from being the strategic reserve to being an operational, deployable fighting force. No longer was the Guard to automatically be considered for protection of public order mainly on the home front and only used as what some viewed as the "junior varsity" force. By March, 2003, the National Guard joined the active duty in Operation Iraqi Freedom (OIF) and for the next decade would operate in the two theatres contiguously. As a reflection of the growing relevance, in 2008, the National Guard Empowerment Act promoted the highest attainable rank in the command of the Guard from Lieutenant General to General Officer. The highest political representatives in the nation banded together in a bipartisan effort to include the National Guard as a coequal branch in the Department of Defense. By 2011, President Barack H. Obama placed the 4-star General William McKinley on the Joint Chiefs of Staff – finally granting the National Guard full equality with the other branches of the military, the United States Army, Air Force, Navy, and Marines. To this day, there have been four four-star generals in command of the National Guard – General McKinley, General Frank Grass, General Joseph Lengyel, and General Daniel R. Hokanson. Under Hokanson's direction, the National Guard continues to serve both in its domestic mission and its overseas national defense role. During Operations OIF and OEF, the National Guard has been an integral part of hurricane relief, wild fire suppression, civil disorder control, and anytime the Governor of their respective state calls them out to perform their duty to protect their fellow citizens – a duty that has not changed in essence since 1636.

This broad overview of the history of the National Guard from the colonial era to present day in the context of Enlightenment principles and significant events in U.S. history sets the stage for a more detailed analysis of why the Deontological argument for voluntary military service is applicable to the

---

[38] GWOT is pronounced JEE-waht.

United States and the National Guard in different time periods. As we have seen, while a Utilitarian "cost/benefit" analysis is appealing, a Deontological, Kantian argument for the Citizen-soldier model of military service can also be applied. This next chapter will show that application in detail as an ideal under the leadership of General George Washington.

Chapter III

General George Washington (1732-1799) and the Militia

&

A Foundation in the Kantian Categorical Imperative as Applied to Militia Service

> A free people ought not only to be armed, but disciplined; to which end a uniform and a well-digested plan is requisite; and their safety and interest require that they should promote such manufactories as tend to render them independent of others for essential, particularly military, supplies.[1]
> President George Washington, "State of the Union", January 8, 1790

In this chapter, I focus in depth on the foundational American military leader, George Washington, as a key figure who exemplifies the moral duty to serve one's nation in a democratic republic founded on the ideas of the Enlightenment as defined by Kant's Categorical Imperative. In this analysis, I will begin with a brief review of how the Citizen-soldier concept emerged along with western democracy. Then, I will look at Washington's contributions to the citizen-soldier ideal during his military career, and leadership of the men serving in the Militias – which will later become the National Guard. These men[2] answered their own calls to serve and, in so doing, paved the way of the National Guard articulating the moral imperative requirements that a duty applies universally, be deemed as fair action, and never involve using men as a means to an end. We speak of an ideal that was not always attained in practice.

---

[1] George Washington, "State of the Union," Federal Hall, New York, NY, January 8, 1790, accessed April 3, 2019, https://www.archivesfoundation.org/documents/george-washingtons-first-annual-message/).
[2] For men they all are -- women did not join the National Guard until 1956, so it is notable that no women play a large part in the early history of National Guard service.

To be clear, the issue at hand is whether the citizen-soldier concept is not only the best operational model in a democratic republic such as the United States, but is also the most fitting moral and ethical *model.*

In order to forge a historical link between the citizen-soldier concept in a democratic republic and the moral law, one need only look as far as the thirteenth century in England and the Magna Carta. For our purposes, the Magna Carta represented the codification of a radical change in the understanding of leadership. For the first time, the unassailable sovereign no longer held power from God. With the advent of the Magna Carta, the seat of power shifted and the liberty and autonomy to pursue one's own happiness vested in the Parliament. Although it would take another three hundred years to come to fruition, the idea was that the Parliament would serve as a representative body of the wishes of the people. Power now pivoted from the divinely inspired sovereign to the hands of the population who, in turn, granted power to their representatives in government. This concept evolved during the Enlightenment and travelled to American soil with the first settlers. By the time of the Enlightenment, such scholars as Thomas Hobbes and John Locke formalized the rights of the people to pursue life, liberty, and happiness. Thomas Jefferson, an avid reader of John Locke and other Enlightenment philosophers -- held the belief that authority to govern vested in the citizenry. The Declaration of Independence, written by Jefferson in July of 1776, has that very sentiment written boldly in the preamble, "We hold these truths to be self-evident, that all Men are created equal, that they are endowed by their Creator, with certain unalienable rights, that among these are life, liberty and the pursuit of happiness".[3]

It is upon this fundamental concept -- that the democratic republic was founded on the recognition of the individual right to pursue one's own life, liberty, and pursuit of happiness and respect for human dignity -- that this argument is based. The philosophy of ethics is traditionally based on two paradigms that do not normally intersect but parallel each other. The first is Utilitarianism as discussed previously. The second is Immanuel Kant's Deontology. While Utilitarianism focuses on the consequences of actions, Deontology focuses on the actions themselves and what *ought* to be done. This is a more obscure argument, but I believe, a wholly valid one. It represents a rare case where both the Utilitarian and Deontological arguments may be used to attain the same goal – to prove that the National Guard citizen-soldier model is the most fitting moral system in a democratic republic. Through a hermeneutical evaluation, two ordinarily incompatible moral theories can find

---

[3] US Constitution, preamble.

harmony.[4] In a way, this argument represents the crossing of language over a chasm between two ordinarily non-intersecting philosophical paradigms – a bridge that forms a dialogical community between the two theories.[5]

Therefore, I elect to use the Deontological argument made by the Enlightenment philosopher, Immanuel Kant. Kant, building a systematic form of morality, based his theory on Practical Reason, or how the world "ought to be". He called fundamental human action a maxim – defined by a goal and a method of obtaining it. The classic example of a maxim is a man's desire for a cup of coffee. In order to get one, he goes to a café. The goal is the coffee; the method is the trip to the café. For a maxim to be imperative, it must be defined by how he *ought* to act. Of the moral imperative *ought,* Kant identified a hypothetical example and a categorical one. The hypothetical can be described in an "if; then", statement. For example, "If I want a coffee, then I must go to a café" – that becomes a hypothetical imperative. For a Categorical Imperative – the "if, then" statement must meet three requirements (I call them prongs) – the Categorical Imperative must be universally applicable, it must be deemed fair to all parties, and it must not use a human being as a means to an end. Because of the stipulations, it is critical to note that the Categorical Imperative is independent of contingency, circumstance, and time.[6] A product of Reason, the Categorical Imperative is often referred to as a "higher duty" because of this ubiquitous and ever-present nature. For Kant's purposes, practical reason was man's ability to determine a course of action based on the unity of experience through sensory input. In other words, "I want a cup of coffee, therefore I go to a café" is an example of practical reason because my course of action is determined by the experience I have had of finding coffee in a café that has been placed within my cognitive reality through sensory input. Practical reason helps me attain my goal to find coffee through the smell of coffee leading me to the café, the visual neon café sign, the clear window through which I can see people drinking coffee, the sound of china coffee cups clattering amidst metal machines venting steam, and the feel of the hot coffee cup in my hand.[7] Lastly, note that the Categorical Imperative, or higher duty, taken to its extreme is the ultimate moral duty and the act of pursuing that moral duty. The Categorical Imperative differs from the hypothetical one because it must meet the three-prong test – universality, fairness, and not using men as a means to an end. In

---

[4] Hans-Georg Gadamer, *Truth and Method* (New York: Bloomsbury Academics, 1960).

[5] Thomas Kuhn, *The Structure of Scientific Revolutions* (Chicago: University of Chicago Press, 1962).

[6] Immanuel Kant, *Critique of Practical Reason* (Cambridge: Cambridge University Press, 2013).

[7] "Immanuel Kant", *The Stanford Encyclopedia of Philosophy* (Summer 2018 Edition), accessed May 2, 2019, https://plato.standord.edu/archives/sum2018/entries/kant/

Kant's system, it is the ultimate act of human freedom in that the fully free, rational man acts morally (as he *ought*) and the moral action is, in itself, an exercise of freedom. Allow me to explain this slightly circular statement. The Categorical Imperative (an unconditional, universal moral law) is a product of Reason (as opposed to experience). Kant's practical philosophy describes how the world *ought* to be – with each man seeking the highest good, or virtue and happiness. When flexing one's full freedom to take action, the resulting highest good is a result of moral action. Therefore, that moral action is a result of exercising one's freedom.[8] Arguably, a person cannot take a truly moral action if it is coerced or forced. Thus, we can trace the thought process from the Magna Carta and the granting of authority to govern to the people themselves; and then, the Enlightenment theory of a right to pursue life, liberty, and property, to the idea in the American colonies of the moral duty to preserve those rights for yourself and for the community. As a citizen in a free society, the moral law defined by Kant in practical reason, meant that citizens *ought* to serve freely, voluntarily, and autonomously to the benefit of themselves and the community.

Here, as in the following chapters looking at the leadership of the National Guard through the next four centuries, my goal is to argue that the citizen-soldier model in a democratic republic meets the criteria of Categorical Imperative and, therefore, is the most ethical model. This model is an ideal. My goal is not to applaud the individual leader, but to apply the Kantian argument for the morally right action as it applies to the leader – and trickled down to the lowest infantryman with a broad cultural effect.[9] Another consideration in looking at the ideal of the Categorical Imperative when discussing the model of the citizen-soldier is to understand that we are not discussing the well-developed Just War Theory as set out by Michael Walzer in his ground-breaking book *Just and Unjust Wars*. Walzer focuses his attention on the moral implications of warfare itself – particularly where they apply to the justification of entry into war and behavior during war. In the case of the citizen-soldier and the Categorical Imperative in a democratic republic in this book, our focus is not on behavior in war but on voluntary service. The Enlightenment ideal of serving to protect the right of your fellow citizens (and yourself) to pursue life, liberty, and happiness creates the environment to render such service as

---

[8] To be sure, this is not to say men always act morally – even when fully free. Kant's Practical Reason is an ideal and the focus of this very book is on the ideal. In the ordinary course of business, men act immorally routinely. The ideal, for Kant and purposes of the present argument, is a question of how men *ought* to act.

[9] Although, based on the chosen leaders throughout this book, it is hard not to applaud them!

universally accepted, viewed by the community as fair, and each man serving as a means to his own end. The eighteenth-century citizen forms the basis of the community and only serves as a soldier when "duty calls" to protect those rights which meet the three prongs of the Categorical Imperative.

The unique military system created in the United States through the early pre-colonial era and the representative local governments produced a man like General George Washington, the first Commander of the Continental Army. Before that, he was a Major in the Virginia Militia actively serving during the French and Indian War. His transition from colonial militiaman to officer in the Continental Army meant that General Washington represented a classic example of the parallel services as they evolved over the course of American history – from the community-based militias to the standing army of the future Federal government. The Founding Fathers inherited a fear of a standing Army, and therefore provided for militias in the state and federal Constitutions – but the existential concern was more than enforced by a more practical one. Before American Independence from Britain, the colonies were separate political entities. The armies of the colonies were not interchangeable and did not cross colonial borders. A "standing army" was simply a practical impossibility in the presence of colonial militias. Not until the colonies formed the nascent United States at the start of the Revolutionary War was an interstate military even a consideration.

I begin with a study of the first great leader of the American citizen-soldier – General George Washington (1732-1799). Although he launched his military career through service in the Virginia Militia, he seems to have embraced no sentimental or affectionate love for the Militias. Having been a militiaman himself, and then the commander of the Continental Army, he was personally aware of the limitations of both. Early in the Revolutionary War, Washington complained,

> A Militia may possibly do … for a little while; but in a little while … the militia of those States … will not turn out at all; or, if they do, it will be with so much reluctance and sloth, as to amount to the same thing. Instance New Jersey! Witness Pennsylvania! … Can any thing … be more destructive … than giving ten dollars' bounty for six weeks' service of the militia, who come in, you cannot tell how, go, you cannot tell when, and act, you cannot tell where, consume your provisions, exhaust your stores, and leave you at last at a critical moment?[10]

---

[10] "From George Washington to John Hancock, 20 December 1776," *Founders Online,* National Archives, last modified June 13, 2018, accessed August 21, 2018, https://

Arguably, at the time Washington made that observation in New York in 1776, the American cause was at its lowest, darkest point and an overall victory seemed impossible. At the loss of New York, the idea of a vulnerable and weakly unified set of 13 colonies taking on the entire British empire was a daunting one – and not likely to succeed. General Washington was notorious for sending dire messages from the front, hoping to convince the fledgling Continental Congress that no good end was near – and, thereby, expecting them to send more men, provisions, and arms.[11] General Washington had been a young militiaman himself in the 1750s while fighting in the French and Indian War (1756-1763) with the British as a member of the Crown's forces. By 1776, he was the Commander in Chief of the Continental Army, now faced with a formidable foe and questionable troops. The times were desperate and no assumption was a safe one.

Given that he was a militiaman himself, Washington's berating of the various Militias by the time the Revolutionary War was in full swing likely came from a practical realization that the loosely connected thirteen colonies were taking on the most powerful standing army and the most formidable global navy in the known world. Washington was fully aware that the colonies were going up against the largest, most successful western superpower of the age. In a Utilitarian sense, Washington's venting and frustration came from an awareness that they could (and perhaps should) lose this war. In a Utilitarian, consequentialist light, the loss of the war would not only be devastating to the colonies themselves but, personally, to anyone convicted of treason. However, from a deontological standpoint, Kant's universal and timeless Categorical Imperative would imply that service in the Militia, for all the Militia's faults, represented a higher duty to which all citizens of the colonies should aspire. Successful or not, the duty to serve the best interests of one's community was universal, fair, and an end in itself – win or lose.

In Washington's experience, he met the imperative through a willingness to serve Virginia as a militiaman early in the French and Indian War (the "Seven Years War" to Europeans). Service was common throughout Virginia. Washington accepted a commission in the Virginia Militia when he was 21 and, through his service, was able to hone his techniques as a land surveyor. Studying at William & Mary, Washington had apprenticed as a surveyor and had been exposed to the gradually more secular thinking of Western European

---

founders.archives.gov/documents/Washington/03-07-02-0305, quoted in Philander D. Chase, ed., *The Papers of George Washington,* Revolutionary War Series, vol. 7, *21 October 1776–5 January 1777* (Charlottesville: University Press of Virginia, 1997), 381–389.

[11] It is important to note that both the Militias and General Washington himself had experience in the French and Indian War and then in the Revolution.

Enlightenment philosophers. According to the President of William & Mary, Lyon G. Tyler, in 1904 as he spoke in front of the *Phi Beta Kappa* Society,

> This [eighteenth century] William and Mary system was a mere colonial reproduction of the higher education system at Oxford and Cambridge in England. It had its foundation in ecclesiastical dogmatism and developed according to a curriculum which permitted little deviation. But there were indications at a very early date of a speedy breakdown and the adoption of more liberal systems….In Pennsylvania the spirit of religious toleration had been conspicious [sic] from the beginning, and in Virginia the State church had fallen into such disrepute that free enquiry was general….[T]he totally changed curriculum at William and Mary evidenced the influence of Dr. Small and his pupil [Thomas] Jefferson.[12]

Strategically speaking, in the mid-eighteenth century, both France and England believed they had a claim to the economically valuable rich lands of Eastern Ohio and Western Virginia. This international conflict of interests prompted Washington's entry into service of the Virginian colony. When conflicts arose, the young militia officer joined his unit and set about defending the interests of the western portion of the colony. The then Lieutenant Governor of Virginia, Robert Dinwiddie (1692-1770) had a commercial interest in the Ohio Land Company and sought permission from King George II (1683-1760) to use the Virginia Militia to find the French forces and remove them. King George II granted permission in 1753. And so, Major George Washington of the Virginia Militia volunteered to set off for the western reaches to scout for French forces. One must bear in mind, that until the end of the Revolutionary War, all able-bodied colonists (Militia or otherwise) served as British soldiers. Therefore, Major Washington's mission to the "forks" of the Monongahela and Alleghany Rivers was to scout against the French on behalf of the Crown and British interests. The French, meanwhile, were also anxious to control the forks of the rivers. While roads provided only sketchy and unreliable methods of long-distance transportation, the rivers provided the most important avenues of commercial and private long-distance travel. For the French, the Monongahela and the Alleghany rivers connected their interests from the Ohio Valley through New York, Ontario, and well into the northern province of Quebec.

---

[12] Lyon G. Tyler, President of William and Mary College, ed., "Early Courses and Professors at William and Mary College," *The William and Mary Quarterly* Vol. XIV, no. 2 (October 1905): 75, accessed August 8, 2018, https://play.google.com/books/reader?id=gCYjA QAAIAAJ&printsec=frontcover&output=reader&hl=en&pg=GBS.PR1

There was good reason to enlist the aid of the local Militia. During the middle of the eighteenth century in colonial America, the Militia represented the best and most familiar force concerning the advantages and disadvantages of the local area. While Great Britain had a foothold on the coast, the French approached the colonies from the north and west. There was a critical third party involved in the struggle for control as well – the Native Americans, who did not unite but served several different sides during the War.[13] Treaties with the natives, earlier expeditions, and natural senses of a right to expand led both the French and the British to believe they held sway over the Ohio Valley. The conflict came to a head when Britain discovered that the Iroquois had treated with the French to bolster their numbers and remain ensconced in the region. Washington, sent as an emissary, returned with a French refusal to budge. However, along with that bad news, he brought enough information on the French numbers, equipment, and force strength that the overall mission was deemed a great success. Washington was never awarded a commission in the British Army but, in faith, the British Army were glad to have him – true to his Militia roots, he knew the terrain, the weather patterns, had local connections, and had learned the importance of good intelligence, provisioning, and local support.

Still very interested in removing the French from their foothold in the Ohio Valley, the Crown sent Major General Edward Braddock and two regiments of foot soldiers. On they marched towards Fort Duquesne on the strategic juncture of the Alleghany and Monongahela Rivers – heavily laden with canon and cavalry in preparation for a siege. The long, sluggish trek toward Fort Duquesne ended in a mutual surprise meeting – the British expecting an ambush but not finding one, the French and Indians not quite in position to meet the oncoming force. When they did surprise each other on July 9, 1755, the "battle" rapidly turned into a massacre. The French, in a camouflaged crescent formation with a large number of Indian allies, easily defeated the cumbersome, large, slow British and colonial militia force as it approached. Braddock's mounts were killed out from under him four times before he, himself, took a round that led to be fatal. In all, the British lost over 1500 troops, almost 450 killed, while the French lost 200 with only eight killed. Washington, through some miracle, escaped suffering only a wicked intestinal virus. Although he put the mortally wounded Braddock on a cart and carried him to

---

[13] As an interesting side note, it is useful to point out that the Categorical Imperative applied to the Native American service to their people as well. Because it is universal by definition, the Categorical Imperative to defend their interests and to not use each other as means to an end further demonstrates the applicability to volunteer service at arms. This idea is resigned to a footnote because my book is about the democratic republic in America and not in the internal political systems of the Native American communities of the eighteenth century.

safety, Braddock died three days later. Even so, Washington emerged as the hero of the day. First and foremost, he reported to Lieutenant Governor Dinwiddie that the Virginia Militiamen fought fiercely and "behaved like Men, and died like Soldiers",[14] while the British regulars "broke & run as Sheep befoe the Hounds, leavg the Artillery, Ammunition, Provision, and every individual thing we had with us a prey to the Enemy".[15] Years later, Washington was complimented by a Native American who remembered the battle and observed that Washington rode his horse like an Indian and could not possibly have been a *British* soldier.[16]

Washington walked away from the terrible defeat at Fort Duquense a wiser military leader – he realized the need for accurate intelligence, for good order and discipline in the ranks, concrete sources of provisioning, and reliable logistical support. He impressed the Virginia legislature and Lt Gov. Dinwiddie so much that the month following the battle, August 1755, Governor Fauquier "placed him in overall command of the colony's frontier defenses".[17] By 1757, Washington was back on the road to Fort Duquense as Commander of the Virginia Regiment. The British Secretary of State, William Pitt, had decided to retake the critical river juncture. This time, Washington's Militia forces answered to General John Forbes. Rather than experiencing dramatic battle strategy, Forbes' forces benefited from diplomatic maneuvering between the British and the Iroquois to their west in Ohio. While marching toward Fort Duquense, the colonial and British forces were surprised to discover that the French destroyed the entire fort with little to no threat from them. That is not to say the British and Virginia Militia did not encounter resistance on the way – they certainly did. But, in October of 1758, the British and Iroquois entered a treaty in which the British agreed to leave the Ohio valley to the Iroquois and their hunting if the Iroquois would remove their backing of the French forces. When news reached the command at Fort Duquesne, with little hope in front of them and the British forces approaching, they decided to destroy their own Fort before succumbing to the enemy.[18] After this successful mission, Washington then returned to his

---

[14] "From George Washington to Robert Dinwiddie, 18 July 1755," *Founders Online*, National Archives, last modified June 13, 2018, accessed August 21, 2018, http://founders. archives.gov/documents/Washington/02-01-02-0168, quoted in W. W. Abbot, ed., *The Papers of George Washington*, Colonial Series, vol. 1, *7 July 1748–14 August 1755* (Charlottesville: University Press of Virginia, 1983), 339–342.

[15] Ibid.

[16] Paul Vickery, *Washington: A Legacy of Leadership*. (Nashville: Thomas Nelson, Inc., 2010), 29.

[17] Doubler, *Civilian in Peace, Soldier in War*, 24.

[18] The British renamed this location Pittsburg in honor of William Pitt. Today the outline of Fort Pitt (Duquense) can still be seen at the rivers' fork.

home in Virginia – to take on the role of a "traditional" citizen-soldier. From his experiences in 1758, Washington learned that a military leader must be able to work with limited resources and obstinate leadership but also that the colonial militiaman brought unique talents to an otherwise alien and displaced force far from its home in Britain. His knowledge of western Virginia through the march to Fort Duquense suited him and his men well. In addition, after the war, as a true Citizen-Soldier, he divided his time between his military responsibilities and those of a gentleman farmer. In January, 1759, he married a wealthy widow, Martha Custis, and adopted her children.

Between the French and Indian War and the Revolutionary War, the colonies suffered mightily under the reign of George III (1738-1820.) Virginia did not escape the burdens of the taxes levied on the colonies by the Crown – and Washington chafed under them along with the rest of the American farmers. It is important to note here, that in a military sense, newly victorious, the colonists had emerged from the French and Indian War with a high esteem of their own abilities to augment the British forces. In turn, given the British reputations for cruel punishments within the ranks, illegally quartering soldiers in colonists' homes, and use of draconian recruiting methods, the colonists did not hold the British regular forces in very high esteem.[19] Through a series of Royal tax acts and other assorted insults, the colonists inched toward a radical concept – revolution and independence. By 1775, the Massachusetts Militia in particular began to arm and rebel. On April 19th, the proverbial powder keg erupted in Lexington – with troops literally racing to Concord, where the "shot heard 'round the world" ostensibly began the American Revolutionary War.[20] The Second Continental Congress, caught up by events, began to look for a leader to rally a fledgling standing inter-colonial army. By mid-June 1775, General George Washington, a former militiaman from Virginia, accepted command of the new Continental Army from the Second Continental Congress. The colonists were uniting behind a common cause that would require both a regular army and the militias of the many colonies.

The Continental Army divisions, who were to undergo a reorganization in 1777, maintained their state allegiances through their names but added Regimental designations as well. This technique managed to distinguish them from their Militia counterparts. In his role as Commander in Chief,[21] Washington realized there were three important attributes he needed to

---

[19] Doubler, *Civilian in Peace, Soldier in War*, 26.
[20] For an elegant, wonderful, and exciting narrative, read Doubler's rendering of Lexington and Concord, Ibid. 29-37.
[21] Ibid., 24. The phrase "Commander in Chief" originated here, when Washington was made "General and Commander in Chief" of all Continental Forces.

enforce for victory: a clear chain of command, unity of mission, and discipline. Additionally, Washington knew from experience that his primary problem would be manpower. Already attempting to organize a set of colonies divided between rebels and loyalists, the diminished population of sympathizers would need every militiaman willing to fight in order to augment the fledgling Continentals.[22] Significantly, the Congress limited the enlistment of the Continentals to one year – a time burden that Washington bore throughout the beginning of the Revolutionary War. As Michael Doubler so wisely observed, "In creating a Regular Army and maintaining a reliance on the militia, Congress produced a dual military system that would come to have a profound and enduring influence on nearly all matters of military policy".[23] The Second Continental Congress enforced civilian control of the military through legislation by literally controlling the appointment of the officer corps. The Congress left the Militias in place and appointed General Washington and twelve other commanding generals over the Continental Army. The Second Continental Congress controlled the purse strings and the nature of the Army itself with relation to the Militias.[24] While the militias answered to the governors of the colonies, the Continental Army answered to the Continental Congress. The significance of this parallel structure rests in its formation and governance by a citizen-elected legislature. True to the United States' Enlightenment roots, control of Militias rested in the grassroots base and, in parallel, so did the Second Continental's Regular Army. Although the legislatures placed the agreement of civilian service in the formal record, the important distinction between that and indenture is that the legislators were locally elected – power resided in the governed, not in the government. In concept and in theory, the entire enterprise from the elected legislature to the inter-colonial Continental Army, to the Militias, to the individual citizen-soldiers was undertaken freely.

---

[22] Here one begins to see the concerns of the army focus on more Utilitarian issues. This fact brings to light the argument I make that the typically disparate moral theories (Consequentialism and Deontology) can bridge their divide. Both theories are in action here – the Utilitarian concept of practical needs and cost/benefit ratios along with the more ideal concept of a higher duty to serve one's community. This contented coexistence of theories is satisfying to see.

[23] Ibid., 48.

[24] In fact, by emulating the Militia system in the Continental Army, the Congress formed a structure that would dictate the relationship for generations to come. In 1903, this parallel structure is codified by Congress in the Dick Act and by 1973 the US military adopts the Total Force Policy that is in full use at the time of this writing. By modern standards the Regular Army (and Air Force) and its National Guard counterparts are intended to be fully interchangeable.

General Washington was the man who forged the initial methods of practical use of the Continental Army and the individual colonial Militias. I identify this as a significant point because we are at the beginning of the evolution of the interplay between a regular, standing Army in the "united" colonies and the use of the Militia. While some blending of the regulars and the militias ended in successful engagements, others ended miserably. (As with any war, each side enjoyed victories and suffered setbacks). I choose to focus here on the Maryland Militia and their service as citizen soldiers specifically because they represent the ordinary mid-Atlantic soldiers who volunteered to leave hearth and home to defend Maryland and their farmsteads. They were not glamorously dressed in fancy uniforms like New York or unusually feisty in their treatment of the British like Massachusetts – to the contrary, Maryland represents the most typical of the colonial Militias. Brave and motivated, they were more traditional like New Jersey or Delaware – willing to answer the call to defend the local community and even other colonies in a united cause, but not large in numbers or ostentation. Ultimately, colonials like those who comprised the Maryland Militia are those to whom I refer when I talk about the ordinary citizen-soldier and the moral law that called them to duty. The Kantian concept of the Categorical Imperative here applied to service as a citizen-soldier in 18th century America must apply to Generals and ordinary folk alike. It is a universal moral law – and must be demonstrated by both general officers like Washington and private soldiers. As I have mentioned, General Washington began his career as a Virginia militiaman himself. Most of the Virginians and some of the Marylanders "cut their teeth" in the French and Indian War in the 1750s. Now, they were asked to reassert their willingness to put lives on the line in order to attain the freedom to pursue the Enlightenment concepts of life, liberty, and the protection of their property. They did this in accordance with Kant's Categorical Imperative – not to say they were inherently aware of it – but that such universal "higher duties" were implicit in their cause.

In Maryland, the Enlightenment arrived with the settlers in the seventeenth century and, as elsewhere, blossomed in the eighteenth century. Just recently, Elaine G. Breslaw has written a short piece on "Enlightened Marylanders: Scientific Interests of pre-Revolutionary Times", in which she outlines the effects of the Enlightenment emphasis on science in early Maryland history through a medical lens.[25] In support of my point in this book as it applies to Militia service, she observes about science,

---

[25] Elaine G. Breslaw, "Enlightened Marylanders: Scientific Interests of pre-Revolutionary Times", *Maryland Historical Magazine*, volume 113, no. 1 (Spring/Summer 2018).

The new scientific interest was partly a result of Isaac Newton's seventeenth-century discoveries ... the world need not be mysterious and unknowable... New discoveries would improve life while promoting human happiness, the major concern of that era. [26]

Although these Enlightenment studies and interests primarily affected the upper classes, they did trickle down into unlikely places within the Maryland populace. By the mid-1770s, freed African American Benjamin Banneker wrote an almanac and analyzed the flora and fauna of Maryland – in particular, he studied the 17-year locust.[27] Also, "William Diggs, of Prince Georges County exchanged grafts of trees with George Washington".[28] As we can see, Maryland advanced in the Enlightenment sciences and in local politics in step with the rest of the colonies. Bearing in mind that one of the "mistakes" George III made with the colonies was to allow them to form their own local governments at arms' length, Maryland had its First Convention on June 22nd, 1774, in Annapolis.[29] Out of concern for the taxation from the Crown and the resistance in Boston, Massachusetts, the Conference resolved,

I. *Resolved*, That the said act of parliament, and bills, if passed into acts,, are cruel and oppressive invasions of the natural rights of the people of the Massachusetts bay as men, and of their constitutional rights and English subjects; and that the said act, if not repealed, and the said bills, if passed into acts, will lay a foundation for the utter destruction of *British* America, and therefore that the town of Boston and the province of Massachusetts, are now suffering in the common cause of America.

II. *Resolved*, That it is the duty of every colony in America to unite in the most speedy and effectual means to obtain a repeal of the said acts, and also of the said bills if passed into acts.[30]

Notice the Enlightenment language – "natural rights" and the "duty of every colony". Because the Kantian concept of the Categorical Imperative is a

---

[26] Ibid., 5.

[27] Ibid., 7.

[28] Ibid., 8.

[29] *Proceedings of the Conventions of the Province of Maryland held at the City of Annapolis, 1774, 1775, & 1776*, (Baltimore: James Lucas & E. K. Deaver, Annapolis—Jonas Green, 1836), 3.

[30] Ibid.

universal duty, I believe that it applies to both a collective and the individual in that, if all individuals behave as they *ought*, then presumably the collective will follow by definition. This ideal concept is relevant as the volunteer legislatures perpetuated the citizen-soldier construct. Although only one example of a colonial response to the taxation imposed by the Crown, Maryland set an example of adhering to a conceptual "higher duty" – one that was viewed as universal, fair, and in the best interest of every citizen of the colony.

By December 1774, the Maryland delegates reconvened in Annapolis when problems in Boston became more pressing. In general, the delegates seemed most concerned with how the oppressive taxes might affect Maryland but also how it might affect Maryland's trading and commerce with Massachusetts.

> *Resolved unanimously,* That if the late acts of parliament, relative to the Massachusetts bay, shall be attempted to be carried into execution by force in that colony, or if the assumed power of parliament to tax the colonies [as a whole] shall be attempted to be carried into execution by force, in that or any other colony, that in such case, this province will support such colony to the utmost of their power.

> *Resolved unanimously,* That a well regulated militia, composed of the gentlemen, freeholders, and other freemen, is the natural strength and only stable security of a free government, and that such militia will relieve our mother country from any expense in our protection and defence; will obviate the pretence of a necessity for taxing us on that account, and render it unnecessary to keep any standing army (ever dangerous to liberty,) in this province: And therefore it is recommended[31] to such of the said inhabitants of this province as are from sixteen to fifty years of age, to form themselves into companies of sixty-eight men; to choose a captain, two lieutenants, an ensign, four sergeants, four corporals and one drummer, for each company; and use their utmost endeavors to make themselves masters of the military exercise: That each man be provided with a good firelock and bayonet fixed thereon, half a pound of powder, two pounds of lead, and a cartouch-box, or powder-horn, and a bag for ball, and be in readiness to act on any emergency.

---

[31] Note the use of the term "recommended". Service in the Militias was strictly voluntary but the word holds a connotation of social pressure, it seems to me. There may have been some tacit expectation of service. My research does not emphasize this as a fact but it certainly seems possible.

> *Resolved unanimously*, That it is recommended to the committees of each county to raise by subscription, or in such other voluntary manner as they may think proper, ... such sums of money as ... will amount to the following sums ... [money listed] ... And that the committees of the respective counties lay out the same in the purchase of arms and ammunition for the use of such county, to be secured and kept in proper and convenient places....[32]

As a matter of point, it is significant to notice in the above Convention resolutions – the emphasis is on the natural rights of man as they were infringed by the Crown taxes on Massachusetts Bay Colony as well as the recognition of the need for each province to have a right to a well-regulated Militia. Of course, in true form of the Enlightenment thinking, the forces were voluntary and a specific dread of a standing, formal army as a threat to liberty was made clear in no uncertain terms. This dread not only represented the Enlightenment emphasis on free will and individual liberty but also the more practical experiences from the French and Indian War that the British regular forces meant conscription, cruelty, and forced quartering in colonial homes. Finally, by July, 1775, the Maryland Convention delegates, having been to the Colonial Convention in Philadelphia, PA, avowed,

> We, therefore, inhabitants of the province of Maryland, firmly persuaded that it is necessary and justifiable to repel force by force, do approve of the opposition by arms, to the British troops employ – to enforce obedience to the late acts and statutes of the British parliament, for raising a revenue in America, and altering and changing the charter and constitution of the Massachusetts bay, and for destroying the essential securities for the lives, liberties, and properties of the subjects in the united colonies. And we do unite and associate as one band, and firmly and solemnly engage and pledge ourselves to each other, and to America, that we will, to the utmost of our power, promote and support the present opposition carrying on, as well by arms, as by the continental associations, restraining our commerce.[33]

Again, note the emphasis on natural rights, the pursuit of life, liberty, and property, as well as the voluntary nature of service to the cause.[34] At its very

---

[32] Ibid., 8-9.

[33] Ibid., 19-20.

[34] Note well, although the Kantian Categorical Imperative in this book is treated exclusively as an ideal – it was naturally not always met. In the case of the enslaved people of Maryland and of women, the natural rights to pursue life, liberty, and property were prohibited.

basic level, the fact that the legislature of Maryland was able to act as a representational government sending its voting citizens to war, literally represented the concepts of the Magna Carta, and the Enlightenment. Although Maryland is but one example of the responses from the delegations to conventions in the colonies, she was indicative of common reactions from the other colonies. Life, liberty, and the pursuit of property motivated the mutual support and the Kantian sense of a higher duty led them to be suspicious of a standing army and willing to rely on the citizen-soldiers whom they outfitted as was appropriate for the mission.

To establish an understanding of Maryland and her contribution to the militia effort during the Revolutionary War in relation to the Kantian higher duty, we digress briefly to discuss Enlightenment theories on free will and their influences on George Washington's peer, Thomas Jefferson. Along with Washington, Jefferson was a student at William & Mary. In *Jefferson and the Rights of Man*, Dumas Malone calls John Locke a member of Jefferson's "trinity of immortals".[35] An introduction to the Enlightenment theories of the day while at William & Mary would have been a likely effect on both Jefferson and Washington. Much like Kant's theory of the Categorical Imperative, Locke argued for a Natural Law that applied to all people (was universal) and indiscriminate. Like Kant's Moral Law, Locke's Natural Law was based on Reason. In his Second Treatise of Government, Locke said clearly, "The state of nature has a law of nature to govern it, which obliges everyone; and reason, which is that law, teaches all mankind who will but consult it, that, being all equal and independent, no one ought to harm another in his life, health, liberty, or possessions".[36] Beside the Natural Law, Locke proposed Natural Rights or entitlements that included the right to life, liberty and the pursuit of property. Natural Law implied an objective moral duty, like Kant's Categorical Imperative, while Natural Rights implied personal entitlements that applied to all men. Inherent in Natural Law and Natural Rights was a sense of free will of the individual who was able to grant his consent to form a government of the community In Paragraphs 128 and 129 of the *Second Treatise*, Locke sums it up by articulating the two powers man retains when abdicating his liberty: the right to protect himself and others and the other to punish crimes committed against the law of Nature. According to Locke, both rights are compromised when man joins civil society. The society itself wields the power to maintain the common good, in fact, it is an obligation.[37]

---

[35] Dumas Malone, *Jefferson and the Rights of Man*, (Boston: Little, Brown, and Company, 1951), 518. The trinity included Bacon, Locke, and Newton.
[36] John Locke, *The Second Treatise of Government*. Mineola: Dover Publications, 2002, 3.
[37] Ibid., 59.

Under this paradigm, the citizen of the established government was, therefore, obligated to serve the community (although the fullest extent of that obligation is debatable.) One could argue that an individual under the Natural Law, with full independence and free will, *ought to* undertake an obligation and commit himself to see that obligation through – including the assumption of punishment if he failed to meet the stipulated end result. Jefferson incorporated this Lockian theory into the Declaration of Independence starting in the very preamble – quoting Locke's Natural Rights almost word for word. It comes as no surprise that later, when looking at the use of the Militia during the Revolutionary War, Jefferson was loathing to call them out. He highly respected the individual rights to remain a civilian in one's pursuit of life, liberty, and property. For Jefferson, it was better to err on the side of individual liberty than on serving the common good. His style of governance led with a light touch. By 1779, Jefferson became the second governor of the Commonwealth of Virginia and, therefore, commander in chief of the Virginia Militia. When routinely asked for more militiamen in support of the war effort, his response was a resounding no. "[H]e regarded militiamen as civilians who had been drawn from their farms and homes to do temporary service in local emergencies. They should not be sent to a distance; they should not ... be kept in armies very long".[38] As one can see, it was with this Enlightenment sentiment from the leadership in the colonies and the Continental Congress that General Washington led the militias into battle, shoulder-to-shoulder with their Continental brothers.

With the war underway in 1775, Maryland rose to the call to duty and by April, events began to pick up a rapid pace. Maryland continued to arm and created a Council of Safety to organize the Militia. The vast majority of early conflicts encountered by the Maryland Militia occurred on water near and around Baltimore, Annapolis, and the Eastern Shore. As George Washington would observe, one of the drawbacks of "taking men from their hearths and their farms" would result in desertions both petty and significant. Maryland seemed to suffer those events much like the rest of the colonial Militias.[39] However, a very successful use of the Maryland Militia emerged as Washington began to take advantage of the flying camp system. Small units of Maryland citizen-soldiers made themselves available to augment the Continental Army at a moment's notice. Unattached to any formal division, these flying camps were versatile and agile. More importantly, they brought with them the traditional

---

[38] Dumas Malone, *Jefferson the Virginian*, (Boston: Little, Brown and Company, 1948), 344.
[39] Clements and Wright, *The Maryland Militia in the Revolutionary War, 15.* Author's note: It is in the desertion rate that we find a practical example of why the Deonotological argument is an ideal.

advantages of the citizen-soldiers with a personal knowledge of the local terrain and population, as well as much needed manpower outside of the borders of the colony of Maryland.[40] By using flying camps, Washington was able to draw on the militia across colonial and provincial lines.[41]

Of course, everything good must have balance – the flying camps that were so important to Washington's army were comprised of men only enlisted as citizen-soldiers for one year and by December, 1776, their time was coming to an end. "The general disillusionment of the winter of 1776 was not confined to the soldiers, but extended to the officers".[42] Two great successes led by the Continental Armies during that dark winter were battles held in New Jersey – both at Trenton and at Princeton. Maryland's Militia struggled to supply men in support of those battles but were preoccupied by their own conflicts trying to keep the Loyalists at bay in the southern counties of the state.[43] The British, realizing the naval importance of the Chesapeake Bay were threatening both of Maryland's shores and kept the Militias occupied in defense of their territories.[44] In this case, the Kantian ideal plays a more practical role, working in tandem with Lockean ideals – being attacked on all sides, the universal need of service in the local militia, the fairness of it, and the end being the protection of one's own land and community (life, liberty, and pursuit of property) clearly pointed to the Categorical Imperative and higher duty of citizen-soldier collaboration.

When discussing the history of the Revolution and the Militia most historians ignore the Battle of Brooklyn. I choose to include it in the discussion because it very plainly lays out the sacrifices the Maryland citizen-soldiers were aware of and willing to make. The reason this battle gets ignored is that, by August of 1776, (barely over a month since the Declaration of Independence was signed) many Marylanders had volunteered to join the Continental Army. I feel free to include it because the soldiers who enlisted came directly from the Maryland

---

[40] Ibid., 18-19.

[41] This advantage is a harbinger of the struggle to evolve a state force like the National Guard when used internationally. Inter-colonial solutions like the flying camps morphed into international solutions like the use of Federal Status (Title 10) and State Status (Title 32). Notice that this is both a Utilitarian (strategic) advantage as well as a Deontological one (the duty to serve your community on a national level, for example when Hurricane Katrina hit Louisiana in 2005, Guard units from all over the country came in support of disaster relief.)

[42] Ibid., 21.

[43] "Bay" pun intended. Also, by May of 1776, the colonies had formally developed independent governing bodies and stopped referring to themselves as provinces. The new term they adopted was "state."

[44] Ibid., 19-20.

Militia and, when disbanded, returned to the Militia. From a deontological standpoint, one could argue they went "above and beyond the call of duty". Fairly put, the Battle of Brooklyn culminated in the loss of New York to the British who would hold the city for the next seven years. General Washington was particularly hard on the Militia saying,

> To place any dependence upon militia, is, assuredly, resting upon a broken staff. Men just dragged from the tender scenes of domestic life – unaccustomed to the din of arms – totally unacquainted with every kind of military skill, which being followed by a want of confidence in themselves when opposed to troops regularly trained, disciplined, and appointed, superior in knowledge, and superior in arms, makes them timid and ready to fly from their own shadows. [45]

I find this comment especially harsh because it was made after the battle was over and lost – without giving credit to the Maryland 400 who, through ferocious and brave battle, had afforded General Washington time to determine the actual number of the enemy in order to plan his tactics. I believe it is important to put Washington's comment in perspective, and not regard it as a general condemnation of the militia model. Washington had just lost New York in the first major battle of the Revolutionary War. It stands to reason that the General realized he was facing the largest superpower in the Western World and one can almost hear the frustration and dismay come through the words of his report almost a full month after the battle had ended and New York was beyond his grasp. Ultimately, the Continental Army (and their Militia enlistees) was lauded for fighting tooth and nail not to lose New York. The British General Charles Cornwallis who, in 7 years would surrender the entire war in Yorktown, fought against the colonial Militia leader General William Alexander (also called Lord Stirling), himself a New Yorker. When the battle was over he famously said that Lord Stirling "fought like a wolf".[46] The worst of the battle for the Maryland 400 took place at The Old Stone House, pictured here:

---

[45] "From George Washington to John Hancock, 25 September 1776," *Founders Online* National Archives, last modified June 13, 2018, accessed August 21, 2018, http://founders.archives.gov/documents/Washington/03-06-02-0305, quoted in Philander D. Chase and Frank E. Grizzard, Jr., *The Papers of George Washington*, Revolutionary War Series, vol. 6, 13 August 1776–20 October 1776 (Charlottesville: University Press of Virginia, 1994), 393–401.
[46] "The Old Stone House," accessed July 27, 2018, http://theoldstonehouse.org/history/battle-of-brooklyn/, Old Stone House, copyright 2016

Figure 3.1: Old Stone House

The Old Stone House in which the Maryland 400 held their rear guard action in 1776.
(Trainor personal collection)

The house depicted in the photograph was

> [r]econstructed from original materials excavated from the site, it sits in downtown Brooklyn. It is where the MD 400 held their rear guard action and were basically wiped out. There is allegedly a mass grave not far from here, but the archaeology has not confirmed anything. The historical accounts also dispute that a burial trench was ever dug, because of the low lying marshlands that would have made this difficult.[47]

General Washington, watching from a distance, was known to have lamented, "Great God! What must my brave boys suffer this day"![48] One can see a version of the quote on the monument in Prospect Park dedicated to the loss of the Maryland 400 in the next photograph, also taken by Mr. Trainor on that same

---

[47] Ryan Trainor, e-mail message to author, July 27, 2018.
[48] "The Old Stone House: Battle of Brooklyn Walking Tour," accessed July 27, 2018, http://theoldstonehouse.org/wp-content/uploads/2016/01/Battle-Brooklyn-walking-tour.pdf

anniversary visit in August of 2015. The loss of the battle and the obstinate willingness of the colonial Militia to fight against the world's strongest superpower of the eighteenth century demonstrates the Kantian ideal of answering the call of a higher duty. In lieu of a Utilitarian greater good for the greater number, the militiamen fought against and despite the odds. They voluntarily fought right to the end. Ultimately, this moral high ground might have been part of why Great Britain lost in the end, even though there were times during the war when the redcoats held the day strategically.

Figure 3.2: Memorial of the Battle of Brooklyn

Memorial to the loss of the Maryland 400 in the Battle of Brooklyn, 1776.
(Trainor personal collection)

Along with background support, Maryland's role in the early Revolutionary War came to a head in the Battle of Brooklyn, when it supplied a large part of its militia soldiers to augment the Continental Army ranks. A point to be noted is that, as manpower became critical, not only did the militia perform its critical functions within their own colonies, but they were also permitted by necessity to cross colonial boundaries. This decision had been made by the Continental Congress at the same time, 1775, that they formed the Continental Army and appointed General Washington as commander in chief. In broad brushstrokes, the Continental Army carried the day in New England and on the Canadian border during the beginning of the war and into 1778. British general Burgoyne suffered a large defeat at Saratoga, NY, which drew the attention of the French, who had long held vested interests in their territories beyond the St. Lawrence. The Battle of Saratoga (along with the earlier Battle of Bunker Hill) are commonly viewed by historians as the two most significant battles that involved the militia as well as the Continental Army. In 1777, British General John Burgoyne came across from Canada with the intent of attacking American from the northwestern corner of New York. Confronted by the Continental Army and militias, Burgoyne was encouraged by a colonial surrender at Fort Ticonderoga. Even so, his forces, comprised of British soldiers, Native Americans, and German mercenaries known as Hessians, were run ragged by poor supply lines and unpredictable terrain.[49] By the time Burgoyne arrived near Saratoga, his forces were almost completely depleted and the Militia threatened him by rapidly assembling "three to four thousand .. in Continental Army and the insurmountable numbers of Militiamen from New Hampshire, Vermont, and New York. This defeat caught the attention of the French who, for decades, had held a vested interest in the Canadian territory surrounding the St. Lawrence seaway and the Hudson. As a direct result of the united victory of the Continentals and the Militia, the French and the Americans signed a treaty that included the French providing badly needed supplies to the Continentals and Militias in the war effort against the British Crown. The British were dumbfounded and soon realized this position was untenable. Rather than keep fighting in New England, they turned their attention to the American south – where they ran afoul of the same lethal combination of Continentals and Militia.

When the war ended in 1783, both the Continental Army and the many Militias shared an equal proportion of responsibility for a profound, if not surprising, victory. While the Continentals were consistent and disciplined, the Militias provided critical backup, reserves, and logistical support. Utilitarian theory and Deontological theory move nicely hand in hand, here – the

---

[49] Doubler, *Civilian in Peace, Solder in War*, 53.

American cause got "bang for the buck" from the Militias who voluntarily fulfilled a higher duty in the face of insurmountable odds. Ultimately, while Washington was critical of the Militia on several counts, he was well aware that both the Continental Army and the Militias won the Revolutionary war standing side-by-side. Washington started his military career as a militiaman and he ended it as the General and Commander in Chief of the Continental Army. He ended his full career in 1789 as the elected President of the new United States who presided over a peaceful transfer of power in 1797. Because of these experiences, he understood the need for both types of service in the new democratic republic. Significant to this paper is the revelation that service in the militia was wholly in line with Kant's Categorical Imperative. While the weaknesses of the Militia force included lack of discipline, lack of experience, minimal drill practice, and unreliable manpower which led to unreliable provisioning, arming, and command structure communication, the Continental Army had its own weaknesses. They were unfamiliar with the territory, they tended to be weakened by a lack of personal investment in the outcome of some battles, and they could over-drilled into obstinacy and unwilling to "get creative". Personally, Washington represented the Categorical Imperative in action as a militiaman himself, and also by laying a groundwork for the future of the Militia over the centuries to come. Both the militia and the standing army method were to be deemed invaluable to the defense and protection of hearth and home – but it remained the citizen-soldier formula that most perfectly embodied the Kantian Categorical Imperative – universal, fair, and an end unto itself.

The argument put forth by this book is that, since its inception as the colonial Militias, the National Guard is the best moral fit for a democratic republic based not only on Utilitarianism but also on a normative argument. A concern over whether General George Washington, as he embarked as the commander in chief of the Continental Army in 1775, approved of the Militias and their performance is not entirely relevant. I chose to use the disparaging quote from General Washington after the Battle of Brooklyn to show that the Militias were not always a bright star in the mind of the General. And yet, as if predicting this argument would eventually be made, John Adams said at the time, "that the militia 'comprehends the whole people...so that the whole country is ready to march for its own defense upon the first signal of alarm'".[50] The Militias were a

---

[50] "From John Adams to Abbe de Mably," Charles Francis Adams, ed., *Works of John Adams, vol. 5 (Defence of the Constitutions Vols. II and III, 1851)*, accessed April 3, 2019, https://oll.libertyfund.org/titles/adams-the-works-of-john-adams-vol-5-defence-of-the-constitutions-vols-ii-and-iii, 5:494. Quoted in Doubler, *Civilian in Peace, Soldier in War*, 41.

grass roots product of a deontological concept and the moral law – service in support of the community and locality of one's dwelling was universal, fair, and did not use people as means to an end. It was a practical reality of life that worked during the Revolutionary War over all eight years. While not flawless, in fact,

> [t]he militia fought the war's opening battles, formed the basis of the new Continental Army, reinforce the Continentals during crucial battles and campaigns, and performed other important auxiliary functions. Throughout all thirteen colonies, Patriot militiamen denied the British control of the countryside, stood their ground against Loyalist militia, and insured political support for their cause. However, the militia proved incapable of prevailing in battle alone against British Regulars and usually failed to provide sustained combat power during independent, extended operations.[51]

General Washington, of all the Colonial military leaders knew the advantages of the Militias and their disadvantages from personal experience. Of particular note, Washington himself had benefitted from the French and Indian War – along with the rest of the Militias upon which he would rely during the Revolutionary War. The experience gained in the 1750s would be invaluable to correct the image of the Militias as "ragtag" – they were hardly that. A significant number of the citizen-soldiers who made up the New York, Pennsylvania, New Jersey, Virginia, and Maryland Militias had served in the northern regions of the western territory. The point, thus made, is absolutely critical to the argument at hand – those who answered the higher duty of answering the call to defend their local community as citizen-soldiers developed experience and abilities that served the interest of the colonies well in the Revolutionary War. Kant's Categorical Imperative, or moral law, was and is truly universal – it is applicable both as a moral duty and as a continuous supporting factor in communal life.

The timeless and universal nature of the Categorical Imperative provides us with an excellent platform with which to launch into an analysis of the National Guard over its 400-year tenure. Given the previously discussed relevance of John Locke's theories of Natural Law and Natural Rights to the actions of the Militia during the Revolution, it may seem that they are the best philosophical framework to apply to the actions of the Guard. It is true that these concepts and motives wove tightly into the Revolutionary War and the desire to rid the colonies of the oppressive Crown control. However, the Kantian ideal, which was also in play, sweeps a broader brushstroke that covers all aspects of citizen-

---

[51] Ibid.

soldier service from 1636 to present day. While the defense of life, liberty, and property has practical limits, the Kantian ideal embraces the contours of individual and collective duty over time and regardless of consequences. Unlike the Lockean governmental framework, the Kantian ideal as discussed here views a broader perspective; it also effectively applies to National Guard service beyond the borders of the United States and can be used to explain the moral duty to contribute to the defense of national interests abroad. In such a case, national interests may include but not be limited to mutual defense forces (like NATO) and international terrorism – which involve the defense of the rights of others. In such cases, one's focus transfers from merely defending a pursuit of life, liberty, and property to a broader scope of the moral ideal "higher duty" of the Categorical Imperative – timeless, fair, and not using men as a means to an end in order to protect mutual interests. Locke, while giving the Founding Fathers a political theory that upended traditional authority roles, handed Thomas Jefferson the metaphorical keys with which to create a democratic republic capable of wielding power with the authority of the governed. This political theory, however, was limited when looking at a higher duty to serve the community in a manner that meets the more apt Kantian Categorical Imperative over time and geopolitical evolution.

Note that the pure Kantian ideal is met through the Militia through voluntary service without the intention to completely submerge the soldier's life in the military. By virtue of being universal, fair, and non-manipulative, the traditional militiaman was a volunteer and not necessarily committing to a life long career. The term "citizen-soldier" refers to that concept in a simple format – the service member is a citizen and a soldier in equal balance and through his own volition. The way that this type of commitment is more purely Kantian falls in the rubric of the universal (everyone has a duty to serve) that is fair (supporting the community and with equal cost/benefits) and without using the individual as a means to an end. The final prong of "means to an end" is met because the service is the end unto itself. Uncoerced and personally beneficial, the service is both the means and the purpose at once. [52] That the service was deemed fair and not a use as a means to an end is part of the application of the moral law. It plays out in the fact that the experiences gained by service as a citizen-soldier became a fundamental advantage to Washington during the

---

[52] The minute one sees "cost/benefit", one thinks of Utilitarianism. Here, I believe that the two usually incompatible moral theories can happily overlap. The cost/benefit analysis of National Guard service coincides with the higher duty of the normative argument. It is, arguably, the motive for the service in both cases – the citizen sees benefits for himself and the community but also understands that he is serving a greater good, and that he *ought* to serve. Again, recall, I do not argue each person does this in the ordinary course of life – I am arguing an ideal.

Revolutionary War, where the stakes to the future benefits of the community were arguably higher. Such an arrangement is an ideal though and, through the unfolding history of the United States and the National Guard, that ideal will and will not be met. However, as will be discussed later, the shortfalls of the actual militias and National Guard to meet this idea do not themselves undermine the validity of the idea or its application to the Citizen-soldier model in a democratic republic such as the United States.

The purpose of shining a bright light on the story of General George Washington, his experiences with the Virginia Militia as a young man followed by his experiences as Commander in Chief of the fledgling Continental Army in victory through the Revolutionary War, also demonstrates the early relationship between the Militia and the standing army in the United States. By doing so, one can witness the original application of the enlightenment concepts in the new country – focused squarely on the Kantian ideal of the Categorical Imperative. Both the Continental Army and the colonial Militias were necessary, working side by side, to accomplish the goal of independence from England. The moral law – which is timeless and requires an understanding of the duty to follow a universal standard, with fairness, and without using men as a means to an end -- was embodied by the service to the colonial Militia. The idea of leaving home and hearth, to dedicate one's life to the concepts of life, liberty, and pursuit of happiness, encapsulated the performance of a higher duty to one's community.

This chapter launched the story of the National Guard of the United States in the early seventeenth century through the tumultuous years of the Nation's birth. Based on the Enlightenment principles in the US Constitution, citizens took part in protecting their vulnerable communities – performing a higher duty as legislated by a duly elected government. As the story continues in the following chapter, focused around General Charles Dick of Ohio, the seminal figure in the transition from the militias to the modern National Guard, the Categorical Imperative and its universal application will become further apparent as the nation expands in territory and undergoes a vast cultural, political, technological, and economic upheaval.

Chapter IV

The Categorical Imperative and the Evolution of an American 20th Century Citizen-soldier Army (1783-1918) General Charles Dick of Ohio

We the People of the United States, in Order to form a more perfect Union, establish Justice, insure domestic Tranquility, provide for the common defence, promote the general Welfare, and secure the Blessings of Liberty to ourselves and our Posterity, do ordain and establish this Constitution for the United States of America.[1]

"To judge our own actions by the same universal standard which we apply to the actions of others is an essential condition of morality".[2] In his scholarly analysis of Kant's Categorical Imperative, H. J. Paton observed that universality is a fundamental characteristic of morality. Universality implies timelessness and imperviousness to circumstances or consequences. While the Enlightenment theory of moral duty espoused by Immanuel Kant remained evergreen, the nature of the citizen-soldier in America continued to evolve through the decades following the Revolutionary War. In this chapter, I will discuss the development of this concept across the tumultuous nineteenth century in the United States and its culmination in the figure of General Charles Dick of Ohio. I will examine how the unchanging, universal standard of the Categorical Imperative applied to citizen-soldier service across these changing conditions.

The Continental Army, consisting primarily of enlisted men who got their start in the colonial militias, went on its way from 1775 and became a standing army in its own right. Although Americans maintained a healthy fear of a large full-time military force, the Colonial governments agreed that organization for

---

[1] US Constitution, preamble.
[2] H. J. Paton, *The Categorical Imperative*, (Philadelphia: University of Pennsylvania Press, 1947), 73.

the common defense was necessary. In light of that skeptical (apparent) contradiction, the individual States partially maintained their sovereignty by keeping their own formal armies commanded by the Governor of the respective State. Through the evolution of the American military – both standing army and National Guard – the Categorical Imperative remained the overarching tenet. The citizenry of the rapidly growing democratic republic continued to enlist for reasons including the protection of their rights to life, liberty, and the pursuit of happiness with universal, fair, and egalitarian measure.[3]As the country evolved from the eighteenth century, through the Industrial Revolution and the Gilded Age, followed by the Progressive Era, the military adapted in parallel.

The young country, emerging from its War for Independence in 1783 entered into a new century that would bring drastic changes in almost every quadrant of life – from philosophy, to art, to society, to communication, to power production, to farming, to Westward expansion and imperialism, to war to peace, to.......the list goes on. Arguably, the Industrial Revolution was the most dramatic evolutionary catalyst of the nineteenth and early twentieth centuries. The United States experienced all the growing pains of a new nation confronted with such rapid and overwhelming change, to which the Militia system was not immune. Not alone in the World, the United States responded to changes in Western Europe ushered in by the Industrial Revolution, with a blossoming of science and Reason-based studies of the cultural milieu of medicine, botany, physics and the forces behind the use of non-man-made power sources such as gas, electricity, and steam. In the United States, the Industrial Revolution manifested itself in a transcontinental railroad, the introduction of gas and then electric light to both the domestic home and the city-street, and steam to power everything from locomotives to subways. America was a country of cities and people on the move – from sea to shining sea and from rural to urban environments. Philosophically, Europe experienced a growth of the age of Reason as well as an emphasis on Utilitarianism. It is at this time, like no other, that a reliance on the citizen-soldier model of military service began to be justified as a cheaper and less threatening form of military organization than the standing army. The Enlightenment tradition of apprehension around the idea of a large, career military was still alive and well – and the Utilitarian notion of a part-time military appealed to the evolving American democratic governments from both a state and a federal perspective. Before being able to evaluate the Categorical Imperative and its effect on the citizen-soldier concept in the democratic republic of the United States, a basic familiarity of those

---

[3] Of course, the concept of "egalitarian" must be kept in context. Women and African Americans were not included in that class.

changing circumstances will help form a basic understanding of the cultural upheavals.

The era following the Revolutionary War and after the cataclysm of the American Civil War can readily be broken into two political movements – profoundly affected by cultural changes in the world and the young nation. Historians refer to the first movement as the Gilded Age that ran roughly from the mid-nineteenth century in the United States to the early twentieth century. The Progressive Era followed the Gilded Age fast on its heels and ranged from the early twentieth century to the United States' entry into and participation in World War One on the side of the European allies. The two ages were a result of seismic cultural shifts that grew out of the Enlightenment reliance on science and Reason. As the study of the sciences bloomed in Western Europe, America kept pace. Roughly speaking, while Europe was embroiled in Napoleonic Wars (1800-1815), a mid-century series of revolutions, and the end of the Ottoman Empire, the people of the United States were on the move – both physically and in society. The Western World, by virtue of discoveries in electricity, light, telegraph communications, and steam power, began to communicate at unheard of paces. Scientific, industrial, and cultural changes did not arise in the American culture *sui generis*. They transited the Atlantic from Western Europe and spread widely by the new wealthy class in America along with a new, large immigrant population that buoyed the lower levels of society with their new cultures. The wealthy elite class was created by a combination of the inventions of the Industrial Revolution and by a young government only beginning to be confronted with the high finance worlds of trusts and corporations. Significantly, the young government espoused policies based on classic liberalism, which privileged the laissez-faire and eschewed taxation and regulation of business. "Robber Barons" became tremendously wealthy – particularly on oil, steel, and the raw materials required to keep the Industrial Revolution running. In turn, some of the Robber Barons became philanthropists interested in keeping their legacies alive. In 1873, Commodore Cornelius Vanderbilt, the railroad magnate, founded Vanderbilt University in Nashville, Tennessee. It is no small coincidence that Mr. Stanford, another railroad entrepreneur, hammered in the "Golden Spike" to connect the railroad ties of the Central Pacific Line and the Union Pacific Line at Promontory Summit in the Utah Territory on May 10, 1869. By 1885, he founded Stanford University in California. By 1890, John D. Rockefeller founded the University of Chicago with funds from his vast wealth garnered in the oil industry.

As we can see from this brief list, higher education in the United States migrated with the people from the original colonies across the country. Through the institutions of higher education, which provided the new American wealthy elites places to put their money for posterity, the philosophy of Western Europe wended its way across the nation and into the cultural fabric of the United States. The Enlightenment, which extended over a century and a half, influenced Western European culture in profound ways and crossed the Atlantic Ocean to the United States in full force. Based on human reason rather than religion, the Enlightenment sought to explain the fundamentals of human nature. Traditionally, moral behavior had been the purview of the Church – but Enlightenment thinkers began to see that mankind, through reason and free will, was able to determine its own moral laws. Immanuel Kant represented the bridge between the two powerful disciplines – that of religion and that of Reason.

After the American Revolutionary War in 1783 and during the next century, the Enlightenment's emphasis on science and Reason hit a high point in Western Europe, acting as a predictor of the dramatic social changes ahead. Although organized religion remained relevant – exemplified by the Romantics like Friedrich Schleiermacher and the Modern Movement of the late nineteenth century and its English counterparts – the Western World rode high on Reason, science, and discovery. The study of the Earth expanded as the United Kingdom, with the most powerful naval force in the world, turned to science for something the Admiralty called the "Discovery Service". Travelling the four corners of the Earth, the Discovery Service encompassed the Globe around the Equator and from Pole to Pole. In the United States of America, the locomotive connected the America from across the 3000-mile span of the continent. During the course of the hundred years from the nineteenth century to the twentieth, electricity united the nation through the telegraph lines. Electricity lit urban streets and changed the face of society as it was able to move from the country into larger and larger cities.

Thus influenced by both European culture and philosophy, the United States responded in kind. In Western Europe, the Enlightenment flowed into a naturalism espoused by the Romantics. The Romantics emphasized an individualism that found its realization in experience. While trying to incorporate God into the Romantic experience, one of the most significant theologians of the Romantic period, Friedrich Schleiermacher identified that very moment when the realization of the existence and quality of an object forms in the human consciousness as the moment of Godhood – a sort of revelation of existence.[4] Kant's transcendental idealism continued in vogue as science began to erode mere religious faith as a source of cause and effect. Kant's theory held that man's perception of objects was not phenomenological (i.e., an awareness of the objects themselves) but was numenological –

---

[4] Friedrich Schleiermacher, "Second Speech on the Nature of Religion", *On Religion*, trans. John Oman (New York, 1958).

impressed on man by an *a priori* "awareness" by the appearance of the object before identification can take place. Once the act of perception is identified in time and space, the object is conceptually interpreted and an image is designed. Realization and conception of an object is a four-part action – sensory input, imaging, conceptual interpretation, and Reason. The continuity of the thought path is what holds the system together and gives the object its context. We base this faculty of perception on Reason in order to explain how they all belong to a single system of reality – the parts fit together in a logical, predictable pattern.

As part of this transcendental theory, Kant's Categorical Imperative remained critical in the philosophical discourse of morality and ethics. In the early nineteenth century, two Londoners, Jeremy Bentham (1748-1832) and John Stuart Mill (1806-1873) developed an alternative moral theory of Utilitarianism. In Utilitarianism, Bentham and Mill argued that ethical behavior might be defined by action that results in the greatest happiness for the greatest number. Also known as "Consequentialism", Utilitarianism relies heavily on the circumstances surrounding the moral decision. Unlike the Kantian Categorical Imperative, which operates in spite of circumstances or outcomes, Utilitarianism based its decision on the greatest benefit for the least cost.

Ordinarily, Kant's Categorical Imperative, a transcendental theory of moral behavior that involves a universal behavior that applies in all circumstances regardless of consequences, and Mill's Utilitarianism, a material theory that hinges on circumstances and consequences, are utterly incompatible. Here, in the history of the National Guard of the United States, I believe one can cross the bridge and reach a common language that may not exactly make the two commensurable but run in parallel toward a similar conclusion. When talking about the Enlightenment theory that creates a universal duty to serve to protect a community's right to life, liberty, and the pursuit of happiness, Consequentialism and Deontology can each be applied and can arrive at the same logical conclusion through different means. With two paradigms that, on face value appear incommensurable, it is of great interest that a dialogical community can logically arrive at the same moral conclusion. It is here, in the nineteenth century and the early twentieth-century tale of the National Guard that the first interweaving of the two apparently disparate theories may be seen most vividly. In the early nineteenth century, the leadership of the United States and the National Guard became enamored of the Utilitarian argument for military service of a part-time, volunteer nature. In the same breath, the Enlightenment ideals of voluntary militia service also underpinned the reasons why men served. In order to protect their homes, their towns, and their states, Militiamen were empowered by the Enlightenment theories upon which the Democratic Republic was founded – and they did so fairly, universally, and so as not to be used as a means to an end. Taking part in the safety of the community in the form of military service was a means in and of itself. Thus, both Utilitarianism and Deontology worked figuratively hand-in-hand. With a nod to the hermeneutics of the twentieth century and Hans Gadamer as well as to Thomas Kuhn, it is very important to emphasize that the 19th Century represents a circumstance when Utilitarianism and Deontology can be spoken of as weaving through each other – or at least running in parallel agreement rather than being at odds. This concept continues to be the case throughout the history of the National Guard. Although we will see that the National Guard authority and controlling forces (both political and military) adopted the Utilitarian argument first and foremost – the actual behavior of the American people was and is more reflective of by the Kantian theory of moral behavior. The two ordinarily incommensurable paradigms do seem to overlap in the case of the Citizen-soldier in a democratic republic.

From a Utilitarian standpoint, the National Guard is definitively less expensive in money, time, and effort from a standing army. As one will see in the next chapter, working on weekends and two weeks a month is significantly less onerous to the nation and the soldiers themselves than full-time career service. Those who are trained only during that time on equipment that is used during the abbreviated training periods save on salaries, facilities, and common wear and tear. For a less expensive military, one gets a fully formidable one (at least in theory.) The Utilitarian argument for nineteenth-century service in the National Guard was not a strong one but grew stronger and stronger over time – especially as the militias formalized and gained in experience. It is much easier for military leaders and politicians to talk in the readily available numbers and cost to benefits analyses of Mill's theory than to argue on behalf of a transcendental universal morality. Nevertheless, the Deontological argument was and remains applicable as its formula lays out – since the Enlightenment origins of the American democratic republic, the duty to serve one's community was viewed as fair, universal, and one that avoided using the citizen as a means to an end The two theories march along contentedly together.

In accordance with the influence in Europe of Kant's transcendental Categorical Imperative and by the Romantic Movement, American philosophy of the nineteenth century found itself glorifying Nature and encouraging individualism by a return to the solitude and self-sufficiency of the wilderness. Ralph Waldo Emerson and his protégé Henry David Thoreau embodied this new, profoundly American school of thought. Along with this return to Nature of the early nineteenth century, by the 1870s, William James established himself as the father of American Pragmatism – a philosophy that espoused Enlightenment Reason as it applied to reality – concerning themselves with the practical use of objects and the ensuing results. When focused on morality, the Pragmatists – in true American form – saw moral virtue as not a means to an end (the third Kantian prong of the Categorical Imperative) but as a goal in and of itself. In other words – action viewed as "moral" need not be a means to achieve an end but an act itself wholly worthy of being taken with disregard of attaining an end.[5] By holding that moral virtue served as its own goal, the Pragmatists aligned with the Kantian Categorical Imperative. The role of the Citizen-soldier was, all by itself, the performance of a higher duty to society without any hint of being used as a means to an end. Voluntary service to the well-being of the community was the goal, in and of itself.

Dramatic changes were taking place across entire cultures and the United States was not immune – the nineteenth-century Gilded Age metamorphosed into the Progressive Era. Along with these changes, the structure of the United States and the military began to evolve. The Gilded Age, so named by Mark Twain, drew its style from Britain's Victoriana – a stiff upper-lipped society where the upstairs and the downstairs classes were sharply divided. Wealth landed in the coffers of a very few while the rest of society dwelt either in cities or rural farmland as America pushed West. Westward expansion met with resistance as the pioneers and railroads encountered Native American tribes already *in situ* and another culture to the South in Mexico. The Army, both the Continental and the restless militias, had to adjust to the rapidly changing cultural environment of the Wild West. Congress, back in Washington, struggled to define the roles of the Federal standing army and the militias. As demonstrated earlier and throughout the Revolutionary War, the fledgling standing army (the Continentals) and the colonial Militias had found themselves fighting side by side. As the war had worn on, General Washington had acknowledged that the two forces had different strengths and weaknesses and managed to consolidate the two – thereby ensuring victory against the larger, stronger, and global "superpower", the British. By 1783 and after, the Continental Congress had set about writing a Constitution of the United States that would leave the two separate but intact entities. However, their compatibility would remain to be seen.[6] To assure the individual states that they would retain the autonomy represented by a local armed force, the framers of the Constitution included in Section One, Article Eight authorization for a well-regulated militia and that Congress must provide for the "calling forth the

---

[5] Writings of William James (1842-1910), Charles Sanders Peirce (1839-1914), and John Dewey (1859-1952) in general.

[6] As a narrative, the struggle between the standing army and the National Guard – rather like states rights versus federal rights – is one that has reached a companionable coexistence but not a verifiable "friendship" to this day.

Militia to execute the Laws of the Union, suppress Insurrections and repel Invasions".[7]

Recall that, as of 1775, the colonial militias were permitted to cross-colony lines in support of the Continental Army's mission. The Constitution made no mention of Militias crossing state lines, so that ability was not rescinded but, interestingly, neither did it mention crossing international lines. So, for the intent of the Constitution, the Militias were state-owned and operated but not intended for international service. The Militia Act of 1792 codified the intent of the Congress. In all, though, not only did this provision acknowledge the rights of the individual states to have a Militia – it directly reflected their Enlightenment roots by appreciating free will, human dignity, and personal sovereignty. The Militias, drawn from the local population, had direct sovereignty over the protection of civil rights and order. In accordance with the Kantian Categorical Imperative – the Constitution, created by elected officials, granted the power to protect life, liberty, and the pursuit of happiness directly to the people of the individual states rather than to a large Federal government that would more likely use men as a means to the end of perpetuating or strengthening its own power. Such a threat had been a valid concern of the Founding Fathers. Certainly, any government, federal or state, could be guilty of abusing the citizen's duty to serve in the defense of the community, but several of the state constitutions mirrored the Enlightenment roots of the federal one. In 1875, the state of Nebraska's Constitution opened with "All persons are by nature free and independent, and have certain inherent and inalienable rights; among these are life, liberty, the pursuit of happiness".[8] Tennessee (after a few iterations ending in 1870) opened with,

> Section 1. That all power is inherent in the people, and all free governments are founded on their authority, and instituted for their peace, safety, and happiness; for the advancement of those ends they have at all times, an unalienable and indefeasible right to alter, reform, or abolish the government in such manner as they may think proper.[9]

---

[7] US Constitution, art. 1, sec. 8.

[8] Nebraska Constitution (1875), art.1, sec I-1, accessed April 3, 2019, https://nebraska legislature.gov/FloorDocs/Current/PDF/Constitution/constitution.pdf.

[9] Tennessee Constitution (1870), art. 1, sec. 1, accessed April 3, 2019, https://www.tngen web.org/law/constitution1870.html.

Likewise, in 1857, Iowa began with

ARTICLE I. - Bill of Rights

Rights of persons. Section 1. All men are, by nature, free and equal, and have certain inalienable rights - among which are those of enjoying and defending life and liberty, acquiring, possessing and protecting property, and pursuing and obtaining safety and happiness.[10]

These are but three examples of state constitutions either written or adopted in the mid-19th Century that are excellent examples of having their roots firmly planted in the Enlightenment; clearly sprouting from the original Federal Constitution in 1789. As the 19th Century United States began to push Westward on the Continent and to push fluid boundaries of territory, the Kantian Categorical Imperative could still be evident in the strong desire of the Militia soldiers to volunteer for service. For at least a generation now, young Americans had served their interests in the military units of their respective states – and the westward push was no different. With a clear reference to the Kantian Categorical Imperative so brilliantly employed by the Founding Fathers, the states exercised their free will to pursue life, liberty, and property in order to protect the common good.

It comes as no surprise, then, that conscription presented a problem for the militias, even this early in their history. Therefore, we must begin to address the problem of conscription and the Kantian (Enlightenment) Categorical Imperative. Before launching into the timeline, an important note must be taken: the Enlightenment foundation of the democratic republic that became the United States in the eighteenth century struggled to balance the need for national security with respect for individual free will, human dignity, and the pursuit of life, liberty, and happiness. The common, unremitting, and underlying theory no matter the outcome was the Kantian Categorical Imperative. That theory was and is an ideal. The United States ebbs and flows in its ability to attain such an ideal – but the goal is universal, fair, and seeks to never use men as a means to an end. Thus, the governing forces within the United States – of the people, by the people, and for the people – recognizes the American Enlightenment culture of service to the hearth, the community, and the nation as a whole. Conscription, on its face, seems to violate the third prong – the use of men as a means to an end; and the Militia Act of 1792 did exactly

---

[10] Iowa Constitution (1857), art.1, sec. 1, accessed April 3, 2019, http://publications.iowa.gov/135/1/history/7-7.html.

that. While the required service of able men from 18 to 45 seemed to violate the concept of "means to an end" – I argue that in the sense of the citizen-soldier, it may threaten the language but not the intent. It is critical to understand that the argument presented in this paper is an *ideal* – that the citizen-soldier model in America is the most moral form of military service in a democratic republic. The National Guard, from 1636 to present day, did not always abide by the citizen-soldier model as espoused by the ideal volunteer supporting his local community.[11] In the case of the Militia Act of 1792, requiring a person to serve in a military force could be interpreted as the state using the citizenry as a means to an end – as soldiers in a war to attain victory. (The means being the soldier and the end being victory). However, there was a critical difference. In the case of the eighteenth-century Citizen-soldier, the man conscripted by the Militia Act of 1792 was a voting member of the population; which elected the Congress who passed the Militia Act that required him to serve to defend his own community. So this requirement cannot be seen as similar to impressment or forced conscription, but as the consequence of elective action by people who have chosen to become or remain members of a republic. He was permitted to go beyond the boundaries of his state but not beyond the boundaries of the new nation that, at the time, was struggling with the Northwest Territories. Militias rarely strayed beyond their borders and fought almost exclusively on behalf of local interests. In other words, the militias were protecting the interests of the communities to which their members belonged, and for whom they voted in a representative legislature, as opposed to protecting the interests of the divinely inspired sovereign who ruled over them.

The first war to test this theory was the War of 1812. Merely one week prior to the passing of the Militia Act of 1792, Congress approved the Calling Forth Act that "specified the manner in which the militia could be used in federal service to fulfill constitutional roles 'to execute the Laws of the Union, suppress Insurrections and repel Invasions'".[12] These two attempts at codification of military service in support of the security of the states as a single united entity represented Congress' recognition of the problems a fledgling country faced when founded on the Enlightenment theories of life, liberty, and the pursuit of

---

[11] The use of conscription always flies in the face of the Kantian Categorical Imperative when the Federal government forces military service upon the citizenry against their will. The resistance during the Vietnam War against the active duty is a good example. In that case, the Federal government of the United States attempted to force citizens into a war they felt was unjust against their free will. Rioting and defection resulted. In the 19th Century in New York we have an example of the Federal government attempting to conscript militiamen into the Civil War, which also resulted in famous riots and resistance.

[12] Marion and Hoffman, *Forging a Total Force*, 4. Quoting the Calling Forth Act of 1792.

happiness. Americans did not then and do not now take their liberty lightly. In the balance, however, hung the very security of the nation. The Kantian concept of the Categorical Imperative to serve runs deeply in the American psyche as evidenced in the preceding chapter, but, although universal, its depths were unplumbed as an inexperienced Congress confronted its first war since American Independence. The question remained open as to whether the militias would answer the call to fight against Britain again only this time as far away as the Gulf Coast. Congress, recognizing this fact, already began to struggle with the fundamentals of military service as a citizen-soldier in a democratic republic. As we will see throughout this book, the struggle to balance respect for individual autonomy while understanding the communal need to protect those liberties begins here in the eighteenth century and runs throughout American history to the present day.

Over the early nineteenth century, through the War of 1812 and a second victory over Britain, the concept of a standing army gained favor in Congress. The Federal government began to recognize the need for an army comprised of career soldiers and officers who would stand ready – equipped and trained -- at a moment's notice. Meanwhile, as society changed from one comprised primarily of rural yeoman farmers to ones in which urban businessmen predominated, and as the division between wealth and poverty expanded, militia service became less and less appealing. The causes of the loss in interest are myriad.

A number of specific problems degraded the enrolled militia's effectiveness and social standing. In general, the States expanded the list of authorized exemptions from military duty available to the wealthy and professional until the working class and the poor perceived militia service as their particular burden. The failure of many state AGs to administer the system also hastened its demise. [13] The position of AG was often the object of political patronage and bestowed upon men with little or no military experience. The compensation and recognition the States afforded the office ranged from the generous to the niggardly.[14]

---

[13] AG is short for Adjutant General, the commanding rank for any State militia force. Today that rank is typically a Major General (two-star) but may be a one-star Brigadier General (no surprise, each state is different – as recently as 50 years ago, Georgia had a Major as an Adjutant General. He refused to wear his uniform to military functions because he was embarrassed to be seen with the General officers of the other states.)

[14] Doubler, *Civilian in Peace, Soldier in War,* 88-89.

Without any method to federalize the National Guard, Congress and the states were stymied when it came to asking citizen-soldiers to cross international borders in defense of the states with a united interest. Since 1775, Washington's Continental Army had evolved into a standing army and was ready at hand for international skirmishes like the War of 1812 and the Mexican Border War of 1846 (brought on by the accession of Texas into the Union). But the standing army was itself a work in progress and insufficient to meet the needs of the country. It needed its ranks augmented by citizen-soldiers who were ready, willing, and able to come to the defense of their country. Soldiers from the Revolutionary War and sons of soldiers found travel, excitement, and adventure alluring and such emotions added to their willingness to form up. Without any formal codification for federalization, however, Congress was unable to authorize such service. When the need arose, Congress decided to ask for "Volunteers" which then placed the state Militias in a status that circumvented the problem – and created, not National Guard companies, but Volunteer forces. Interestingly, in the course of the early nineteenth century, two parallel "volunteer" armies began to develop alongside the Continental Army created in 1775 and led by George Washington. The "old" Militia system began to sink under the weight of a growing disparity of wealth and poverty. Those who could afford to took advantage of state-enacted deferments from service while the poor began to view service as a burden. In the meantime, however, unofficial volunteer state "Militias" became popular as community resources – and seemed to fill the void left by the collapsing original militia system. By 1825, a New York State volunteer force began to call itself the National Guard. As homage to the Marquis de Lafayette and his tremendous support during the Revolution, this New York volunteer unit was the first formal group to adopt the anglicized version of La Garde Nationale – the name for the French army.[15] During Lafayette's return tour of the United States in which he covered over 4000 miles of territory, New York honored him with several parades, plenty of pomp and circumstance, and the re-naming of the New York State military organization to the New York Battalion of National Guards.[16] What could be more flattering to the Marquis than to name the New York militia after his homeland's army? The name "national guard" for the original colonial Militias became standard usage throughout the young nation but was not formally codified until the twentieth century – a story encapsulated in this chapter.

Based on a good understanding of seismic cultural changes in the nineteenth century, a philosophical analysis of the Categorical Imperative and the Citizen-

[15] William Swinton, History of the Seventh Regiment, National Guard, p. xx.
[16] Doubler, *Civilian in Peace, Soldier in War,* 95.

soldier in a democratic republic barrels forward. As I focus on military service in this era, three major threads exist that we can follow with relative ease. First, there is the evolution of the militia structure from the colonial design to the new state Volunteer militias. Second, is the rise of civil disorder brought on by the change in labor and the Industrial Revolution and the role of the National Guard quelling labor disputes. And, third is the blossoming Imperialism as the frontier closed and the fledgling country began to look beyond its borders. All three of these trends touch on the cultural application of the Categorical Imperative by demonstrating how its universal nature, fairness, and proscription of using men as a means to an end continued to influence the Guard through the nineteenth century.

The pivotal period of the 1890s to early 1902, the Gilded Age -- a time of rugged individualism, the allure of the cowboy, the Social Darwinism that insisted on "survival of the fittest", and the stark dichotomy between the working class and the socially distant upper-class elite -- gave way to the Progressive Era. The clearest illustration of that pivot was through the lens of the politics of the Executive Branch. President William McKinley (1843-1901) served in office from 1897 until his assassination in 1901. A former Ohio Governor, McKinley led the United States and the National Guard through its first war since the Civil War – one that took place in an international theatre. Critical to that endeavor, a man named Charles Dick would forever change the future of the National Guard as it was then known. Fellow Ohioans, Dick and McKinley knew each other and were known to converse in private via a "new-fangled" machine, the telephone. In fact, Senator Dick's great-grandson specifically noted in an interview, "He was one of McKinley's closest advisors and was said to be the go-between to the Army and the Navy high command".[17] When McKinley was assassinated, his Vice President Teddy Roosevelt, a force of nature unto himself and a veteran of the New York National Guard, embodied the transition from the Gilded Age to the Progressive Era. If a buzzword exists for the Progressive Era, it should be "reform". The excesses of the Gilded Age in the country's youthful exuberance spread across the continent and entered the global stage economically, militarily, and culturally, but had ignored the working class. The elite of the Gilded Age had rationalized the existence of the working poor as examples of Social Darwinism at work – they were simply inferior and unable to support themselves; or had heeded Carnegie's almost Aristoltean encouragement to help the working poor as part of their philanthropic social responsibility. Ultimately, the unregulated capitalism of

---

[17] Charles Tharp, great-grandson of Charles Dick, answers to questionnaire written by author, Washington, DC, August 20, 2018.

the Gilded Age seems to have been the root cause of the immiseration of the working poor.[18] The Progressive Era aimed to tame "rugged individualism" and to create a social safety net to the tune of "safety in numbers". Associations, Labor Unions, and united movements sprang up across the country. One association in particular was critical to the nature of the evolution of the National Guard but first, a moment must be spent on the politics of the transition from the Gilded Age to the Progressive Era. Roosevelt assumed the Presidency with an agenda – one undoubtedly colored by his own service in the National Guard in the Rough Riders during the Spanish American War (1898). Roosevelt spent his tenure fulfilling his promise of a "Square Deal" for the American people. The "Square Deal" focused on food and drug regulation, railroad regulation, trust-busting and generally expanding the Federal government's role in the lives of private citizens for the public welfare. If a simple statement may sum up the change in the two eras, while the Gilded Age applauded the rugged individual, the Progressive Era championed the legitimate role of the federal government in protecting the safety, health, and rights of the private citizen. The development of the association that would impact the evolution of the National Guard from 1878 to present day was indicative of the Progressive Era's drift away from rugged individualism and move toward collective interests (or "safety in numbers", really.) In 1878 during post-Reconstruction, several general officers of the Militias realized that the militias would need representation in Washington, DC in order to protect the state soldiers and to ensure the government met their needs. In fact, two separate associations formed – one in the Northern industrial states and one in the Southern agrarian states -- but by 1879, they united to hold the first conference of the National Guard Association of the United States that convened in St. Louis, Missouri. The first President of the Association, General George Wood Wingate served in the New York National Guard and was a strong proponent of rifle marksmanship and safety.[19] Following the long tradition in New York of the citizen-soldier coming from the legal community, Wingate had a strong allegiance to militia service existing alongside a civilian professional calling as a lawyer. True to the Citizen-soldier ethos, Wingate steered the National Guard Association of the United States in an early Progressive course toward protection and advocacy for the well-being of its members. The

---

[18] I am not an economist. I do not intend to sit in judgment of capitalism. It seems to me that the American economic system of the Gilded Age was unprepared for such rapid growth and global change brought about by advances in science and technology. There is quite a difference between a feeble reaction when confronted with drastic upheaval for the first time and behaving in the same laissez-faire way when experiencing it for a second or third time.

[19] In 1871, he founded the National Rifle Association.

Categorical Imperative of fairness, universality, and not using men as a means to an end was personified by the formation of the Association. In many ways, this Association – like others – was formed by a communitarian impulse based on reciprocity. The membership, comprised of National Guardsmen, benefitted from the advocacy the Association provided. But, as an observation, another motive may reasonably be construed as the Progressive realization of the need to support those who contribute time, effort, and possibly the ultimate sacrifice to the needs of the community.

Also in the post-Reconstruction era, the Industrial Revolution and the gulf between the Gilded Age elite and the working class brought about labor conflicts. Working conditions in the factories, mines, railroads, and steel mills were thoroughly unregulated and workers were left unprotected. In 1877, the country descended into a series of violent and chaotic labor strikes. "The Great Riots of 1877 marked the first extensive use of the militia in industrial conflicts.[20] In 1877, requests from nine states came for aiding the local militias in strike-breaking – including Maryland, Pennsylvania, and West Virginia.[21] Over the next several years, the state Governors brought in the militias and federal troops to quash strikes. These call-ups included duty for mining strikes in Idaho and the disastrous Pullman railroad Strike in Illinois. In 1878, Congress enacted *Posse Comitatus,* the fundamental law devised to establish the use of the militias by the state Governors and by the federal government. Under the law, the federal army could not (and cannot to this day) be used to enforce local state laws. Neither the Militias nor the federal army could be granted police powers. Congress drew a bright line between military might and the constabulary within the borders of the United States. This distinction harkens back to the Founding Fathers' fear of a large standing army on the continent that could impose the will of a strong sovereign and infringe on individual liberties, but also to the federalist idea that local disputes between local parties should be handled locally. The reader may see the evolution of the Enlightenment concepts as the country expanded and its role in the world of sovereign nations became more complicated.[22] *Posse Comitatus* represented the Categorical Imperative in action as it invoked principles of fairness and universality by protecting the people from unfair use of the National Guard by the state. It protected against unfairness of arbitrary state power without

---

[20] National Association of Attorneys General, *Legal Issues Concerning the role of the National Guard in Civil Disorders: Staff Report to the Special Committee on Legal Services to Military Forces,* 26.

[21] Ibid., 48.

[22] Ibid., 55. It is important to note, that while the labor strikes shone in the spotlight, race riots also broke out. The first significant ones occurred in the summer of 1919 in Washington, DC, Chicago, Charleston, SC, Longview, TX, Knoxville, TN, and Omaha, NE.

preference to locality, social status, or other circumstances. By so doing, *Posse Comitatus* inherently prevented using men and soldiers as a state-wielded means to an end by proscribing use of the National Guard to pursue state interests.

Washington, DC politics kept moving, and in 1908, Roosevelt encouraged his Vice President to run for office and William Howard Taft became the 27th President of the United States. However, Taft did not meet with Roosevelt's approval and in 1912, Roosevelt split the Republican Party by running on his own Progressive ticket against Taft. The resulting weakness in the party allowed the Democrats to take advantage and that year, President Woodrow Wilson (1856-1924) was elected to office. By 1916, Wilson had sent the National Guard to the Mexican Border engaging in the Punitive War – which set them up for readiness when the United States entered the First World War in April of 1917. The Punitive War of 1916 in Mexico began as a reaction to incursions of Pancho Villa's forces across the border into the Texas Territory. Mexico, during these years, suffered a revolution in which Pancho Villa rebelled against the established President of Mexico, Venustiano Carranza (1859-1920). In response, the volunteer National Guard forces (including the fledgling aviators from New York) amassed on the border with the intention of pursuing Pancho Villa into the sovereign territory of Mexico. President Wilson charged General John J. Pershing (1860-1948) with command of the American forces that included both members of the federal standing army as well as National Guardsmen from across the country. The legal problems brought to light by the international nature of the Punitive War created fertile ground for recodification of Volunteer status when in military duty. Also, notably, it primed General Pershing and his men to move directly from the Punitive War, which quickly was resolved by diplomatic communications, to the combat in Europe the following year. This foundation of the narrative is critical for the reader to understand the social and political environment that formed the crucible in which the nineteenth and twentieth Century National Guard adapted and grew.

One must note that in the military theory of the day, Major General Emory Upton was very influential – if on the short end of how the narrative would ultimately play out. Strongly influenced by his experiences in the Civil War and his love of the structure of the German army, Upton sought to end the dual military forces, a regular standing army and a militia, in America. He "had become convinced of the limited value of militia unless it was kept under the close supervision of, and subordinate to, Army regulars".[23] But more damning, he lost sight of the power of the Enlightenment in the American ethos and "[h]e

---

[23] Ibid., 10.

also underestimated the power of the traditional American belief in the militia concept and the fear of large standing armies".[24] Even though the Kantian higher duty, so infused in the American military mind (and the civilian willing to volunteer to support the community), was not on Upton's metaphorical radar and his theories did not come to fruition, he was still very influential and for several years he was a driving force behind nineteenth-century American military theory and practical structure. For example, as Marion and Hoffman rightly point out, during the initial phases of the Spanish-American war, the regulars were the first to be called up.[25] This very Uptonian model, however, was unable to supply the required manpower. Calling upon the Militia, but aware of the thorny legal issues of sending them overseas, McKinley recruited 200,000 "volunteers" and redesignated the National Guard units with new names. The most famous of the "volunteer" units, the Rough Riders, provided Teddy Roosevelt, one of America's favorite sons, his first taste of military service.

Fully immersed in this milieu, the man poised to enact the greatest change to the face of the growing state Volunteer militias (that became the framework of the modern National Guard) was Charles W. F. Dick. Born in Akron, Ohio, in 1858, Dick grew up in a German immigrant household. On the shelves of the National Guard Memorial Library, the Charles W.F. Dick collection contains several of his childhood primers that are steeped in a morality based on Christian worship. An almost Kantian sense of fairness and an open-handed lack of manipulation are liberally sprinkled throughout the Washington Irving and Benjamin Franklin quotes. It may fairly be observed that, whether he knew it or not, Dick was a Kantian himself – based on his life-long service to his country through the Ohio National Guard, through his representation as a Congressman and then Senator and his presidency of the National Guard Association of the United States. Individual service and circumstance-based benefits from his legal career and business acumen with the Goodyear Rubber and Tire Company served his wallet well, but his military career in the Guard and his long legacy of public service speak clearly to a sense of universal fairness and sense of duty to community apart from any personal benefit he derived. Like the paradox of doing public work because of a sense of a higher duty, not because it makes one liked, does tend to make one liked – Charles Tharp emphasized in his interview that his great grandfather acted through a sincere sense of selflessness with a true love of the National Guard. "Charles

---

[24] Ibid.
[25] Ibid., 11.

Dick believed in Duty, Honor, Country. Above all else....He was for 65 years a tireless advocate for the Guard. In and out of high office". [26]

Charles Dick, born in the Gilded Age and living through the Progressive Era, embodied both cultures. A well-educated lawyer, Charles Dick was a very wealthy man. Benefitting from the Brazilian rubber glut of the 1890s, Dick skirted the traditional Gilded Age elite as one of the largest shareholders and a member of the Board of the Goodyear Rubber and Tire Company. The Industrial Age inventions not only rendered the transport of the rubber feasible but also provided inventions that demanded the rubber for manufacturing. Of course, as Dick served in the Ohio National Guard first as a Lieutenant Colonel in the Spanish American War and then as the Adjutant General of Ohio, he saw a perfect venue for rubber usage in the military. As the standing army and the militias began to adopt the use of mechanized vehicles, rubber was needed for everything from washers to tires to hoses. Charles Dick ended his military career as the Adjutant General of Ohio with the rank of Major General (the Adjutant General is the title of the commanding general of a state or territory and answers directly to the governor of the state). It was this connection, and his connections with President McKinley, that positioned him perfectly to answer the call of fixing the relationship of the National Guard with the standing army and to begin the many year formulation of legislating the legality of National Guardsmen in wartime service beyond American borders.

Well-educated in Ohio, Charles Dick read for the law and he became a public figure in the Republican Party in 1886 when he was elected to be Summit County Auditor. According to his great-grandson, Charles Tharp,

> General Dick joined the 8th Ohio Volunteer Infantry [Regiment] in emulation of the older generation of Ohioans who had fought in the Civil war. At his young age [27] I doubt that he had any foresight of how useful it would be in making friends and winning in politics. I think it was a pure patriotic impulse.[27]

True to the Enlightenment Kantian foundations of the American military, Charles Dick impressed upon his family that he enlisted voluntarily and with a patriotic sense of service to community. While practicing law in civilian life, Charles Dick soon rose to the rank of Lieutenant Colonel and found himself in command of the Ohio Volunteer Infantry (OVI) in the Spanish American War of 1898. Seeing the last remnants of Spain in the Western Hemisphere – or a totally independent Cuba -- as a threat to the rapidly expanding commercial trade

---

[26] Charles Tharp answers to questionnaire by author.
[27] Ibid.

interests of the country, and morally outraged by sensational new articles exposing Spanish colonial rulers for burning farms and rounding up Cuban peasants into camps where they became starving "reconcetrados" the United States declared war on Spain in order to roust them out of their island foothold. Ensuing events, including the controversial sinking of an American ship, The Maine, in Havana harbor resulted in an American declaration of war against Spain – a war to be fought entirely on Cuban soil.

Since the Civil War, the militias of the states had been busy on the Mexican Border during the events of the annexation of Texas into the Union in 1846 and covering the disorder and mayhem brought about by the Plains Indian Wars as the population moved ever Westward and encroached on Indian territory. After the connection of the railroads in Utah Territory in 1869 and the ability of the telegraph to shorten time and distance, the country was now able to claim land from the Atlantic coastline to the Pacific. By 1898, the United States was flexing its muscles beyond its now established borders. During the Spanish American War (referred to by Dick as the War with Spain), [28] Dick "stayed in for the camaraderie and what he learned about military methods, tactics, and strategy...He told his family that his times in the Guard were among the happiest of his life".[29] Lt Col Dick's role in the war was typical of a volunteer Militiaman and he spent the majority of his time behind lines. The question of just exactly how militiamen, not in service to the Nation as a whole but only in service to their respective States, could legally travel and enter combat overseas, was an issue that would land squarely in front of Charles Dick's feet in the halls of Congress.

Following the War, and upon his return to Ohio, Dick was elected to serve in Congress where he became the Chairman of the House Committee on Military Affairs. By 1903 and with his sponsorship, Congress passed The Dick Act -- one of the most significant acts in the history of the National Guard. Also by 1903, the Uptonian view of eliminating the dual military path of militia and standing army became less practical as demonstrated by the Spanish American War of 1898 and the Philippines Insurrection in the Pacific. Both military ventures required the limited regulars be augmented by the more numerous militiamen. Insufficient regulation, however, allowed the militiamen to legally travel with military status beyond the borders of the United States. (Recall that during the Revolutionary War, a special dispensation had to be made for them to travel across even their own state borders).

---

[28] Ibid.
[29] Ibid.

In 1898, Dick was elected to the House of Representatives and in 1904 became a Senator from Ohio. According to his great-grandson, he was the perfect man in the perfect place to orchestrate the passage of the Dick Act (or the Militia Act of 1908).

> The reason that General Dick was in a unique position in 1903 to write and lead in passage of the Dick militia bill was that he was the one man in Washington who had a foot in all camps of the stakeholders in the old militia system, the federal army, the Congress and the White House.[30]

Tharp notes that during the Civil War and the Spanish American War, the state militias seemed untrained and disorganized. The General Officer Staff in Washington, DC felt that the state Governors had too much control over their own Militias. "General Dick", he said, "was in the perfect position to moderate competing interests. As Chairman of the House Committee on Militia [sic] he was at the right place at the right time".[31]

Acknowledging his great grandfather's quarter-century of service, Tharp points out that all of the competing interested parties trusted him with organizing the structure of the National Guard with an eye to the needs of the entire country. Dick was trusted by the Guard, the Governors, and the Executive Branch (Roosevelt included as they had met at the GOP convention of 1880). In fact, the Secretary of War, Elihu Root (1835-1937) asked for Charles Dick by name to lead the committee.

> Charles Dick set to work mollifying all sides, keeping the Guard units under state control, with the Governors appointing the Adjutant-Generals, but subject to overcall by the President if needed for national emergencies. He outflanked the local politicians with the leadership of the President. He got the guardsmen better pay. And he appealed to the General Staff with uniform training and their being able to call on the Guard in national emergencies. And he went out of his way to get better funding and facilities for the regular Army, including West point....Altogether it was a masterful performance.[32]

Like General George Wood Wingate before him, General Dick personified the Categorical Imperative as he served both the people of Ohio in the Congress and then as the President of the fledgling National Guard Association of the

---

[30] Ibid.
[31] Ibid.
[32] Ibid.

United States (1902-1909). That, combined with his service in the Congress, made him the ideal Citizen-soldier to navigate the Militia Act of 1903, named for him, through the governmental system and into good Law. The fundamental impetus of the Dick Act was to protect the interests of the ordinary Citizen-soldier and to begin codifying service requirements, the supply of proper equipment and provisions, pensions and benefits, and duty status. By so doing, the Dick Act codified the Categorical Imperative into action – execution of the universal duty to serve community and country by protecting the soldiers from being misused as a means to an end.

"The Dick Act's major impact was establishment of the principle of providing federal funds and equipment in return for greater control over Guard training and organization, a trend that would continue in the long term".[33] General Charles Dick, never losing sight of his military career, soon became the Adjutant General (or commanding general) of Ohio and the President of the National Guard Association of the United States. The two acts in 1908 and 1916 that followed the Dick Act amended it and created the powerful series of Acts that allowed the federal government to activate or "Federalize" state militiamen. Thus "Federalized" the National Guard could follow their standing army peers to the four corners of the Earth in the interests of the Nation as a whole. On a more subtle but (as time would tell) much grander scale, the Dick Act and the two that followed it, made it clear to the Congress that it was intending to grant the National Guard a parallel evolutionary path with the standing army. In order to serve as equal to the standing army, the Guard would require the same equipment, the same training, the same weapons, the same uniforms, patches, rank structure and – most importantly – benefits and pay. The Dick Act created the now-familiar structure of weekend service once a month and two weeks in the summer for formal training over a continuous period. The critical takeaway from the passage of the Dick Act was the authority of the Federal government to fund the National Guard as a separate military entity from the standing army. Such a financial arrangement honored the Founding Fathers' intent of limiting a standing army by supporting the community-based militias but also rendered the militias beholden to maintaining a federally mandated standard of conduct. Equipment, training, recruitment, and professional education all earned Federal financial support. The Dick Act also affected the standing army – putting the Army on notice that (in a Utilitarian sense) they had better be efficient, capable, and lethal, because, by definition, the National Guard was a cheaper option.[34]

---

[33] Marion and Hoffman, *Forging a Total Force,* 12.
[34] One can see clearly here how tempting it was for the military to grasp the Utilitarian argument for the existence of the National Guard.

By 1916 the Mexican Border War (or the Mexican Punitive Action) drew more militiamen into service. More significantly, however, the war in Europe had been raging since August of 1914. This brutal war extended beyond the continent and began to impact the United States on the high seas through German submarine threats to U. S. shipping and passenger transport. By 1916 it became apparent that the United States would likely enter the war on the side of the Allied Powers. Congress soon passed the National Defense Act of 1916, part of which amended and enhanced the Dick Act of 1903. The Federalization of the National Guard was formalized. "Henceforth, officers and enlisted men...took oaths to both their state and the nation, swearing to protect the U.S. Constitution and obey the orders of the president, which ensure the legality of overseas federal service".[35] Put another way,

> The statute expressly provided that the Army of the United States would include, not only the Regular Army, but also the National Guard *while in service of the United States.* (Consistent with Articles I and II [of the U. S. Constitution]. This act required all Guardsmen to take a dual oath to obey the President and the Governor, and authorized the President or Congress to 'draft' (today we would say mobilize) the National Guard for active duty service.[36]

As amended by the National Defense Act of 1916, the Dick Act's codification of state duty was augmented to correct the lack of direction when the Federal government sent Guardsmen across international boundaries. Specifically, in Section 58, the National Defense Act of 1916 formally recognized the National Guard of each state, territory, and the District of Columbia but went on to create an entity known as the National Guard of the United States. This body "shall be a reserve force of the Army of the United States and shall consist of those federally recognized National Guard units...who shall have been appointed" the Act stated.[37] These soldiers, when on domestic territory, would be trained, organized, and commanded by their respective states.[38] Thus, the Categorical Imperative – a universal duty – began to stretch farther and farther from the local community. No longer would the individual states have to play fast and lose with militia status in order to send their soldiers beyond the borders of the United States. The powerful significance of the National Defense Act of 1916 lay

---

[35] Marion and Hoffman, *Forging a Total Force*, 14.
[36] Donald P. Dunbar, "Legislative History of the National Guard" (lecture, National Guard Association of the United States, Washington, DC, November 16, 2018).
[37] National Defense Act of 1916 (approved June 3, 1916, as amended January 1, 1942), sec. 58.
[38] Ibid.

in the implicit recognition of the Kantian Categorical Imperative embedded in the U.S. Constitution and the American culture – the soldiers now could volunteer to serve their communities and their states as well as serve overseas to fulfill their moral duty as citizens to the nation as a whole. This is not to say each individual soldier served out of a pure sense of moral duty – not at all. The Kantian Categorical Imperative is an *ideal*. One can still argue that the Categorical Imperative underpinned the model of the Citizen-soldier volunteer service and that many volunteers served out of a sense of Kantian duty. It is critical to understand that the fundamental role of the National Guard as a local, community-oriented service based on "voluntary, fair, and an end in itself" theory was maintained. By the declaration of war in April, 1917, "[t]he War Department filled the ranks of the regular Army and the mobilized National Guard largely with volunteers, while directing most draftees to the newly formed divisions called the National Army".[39]

Along with developments in the relationship between the National Guard and the standing army, the Industrial Revolution ushered in a completely unexpected and different aspect of the pursuit of modern warfare. Another example of the Categorical Imperative at work in the early formation of the National Guard appeared in New York with the invention of the "flying machine". The Guard during the early twentieth century experienced a bit of a renaissance when members began to notice advances made in aviation. Among the inventions of the Industrial Age in the late nineteenth century that would change the world, aviation in the United States began in Kansas, Ohio, and North Carolina. By combining the mechanical engine, rubber for tires, and a set of wings, humans were was able for the first time to sustain powered flight. By 1908 the Army accepted its first airplane from the Wright Brothers. By 1912 the New York National Guard had formed the 1st Company Signal Corps at the Park Avenue Armory in New York City, having bought an airplane for $500.

The real introduction of aviation into the National Guard, however, came in 1915, Captain Raynall Cawthorne Bolling (1877-1918) formed the 1st Aero Company in Minneola, New York. Bolling exemplified the citizen-soldier and the idea of voluntary citizen service as a duty to be pursued regardless of consequences. A quintessential American citizen-soldier, Bolling was born in Arkansas during Reconstruction. He graduated from Harvard College in 1900 and then from Harvard Law School two years later. He then set out on his career as a corporate lawyer for Carnegie's company, U.S. Steel, in Manhattan. Like other Americans associated with that milieu, Bolling was financially very

---

[39] Marion and Hoffman, *Forging a Total Force*, 16. Amusingly, Marion and Hoffman point out that even the draft, called "*selective service*, helped soften the reality of for an American public traditionally opposed to coerced military duty."

successful. That success allowed him to pursue his passion for aviation. Bolling, by virtue of his circumstances afforded by the Gilded Age, was able to independently develop his interest in such a significant pursuit. While the circumstances were not necessarily open to everyone, Bolling's interest in aviation could be advanced without the impression that he was being used as a means to an end. The pure enthusiasm for flying and the opportunity to pursue it led directly to the formation of a legitimate military application. The Categorical Imperative, while perhaps not on the tip of everyone's tongues, was certainly in operation during Bolling's career – from genial camaraderie, adventure, and discovery on the fields of his manor house in New York as well as on the fields of France during World War One --fields from which he would not return. It is significant to note that, while perhaps a conscious sense of moral duty was not a part of Bolling's motivation, the resulting benefits certainly fall in line with the application of the Categorical Imperative. On November 19, 1916, ten JN-4 ("Jennies") flew from Minneola to Princeton, New Jersey – successfully completing the largest formation military flight in U.S. history up to that date. By 1916 the 1st Aero Company was the first unit to be Federalized and called into service for the American interest in the border conflict with Mexico. By the end of 1916, the Federalization of the National Guard would be formally enacted. On April 2nd, 1917, President Woodrow Wilson asked the Congress of the United States to declare war on Germany. On April 3rd Bolling volunteered in the Army. He entered the Signal Corps and eventually assumed the role of the Assistant Chief of the Air Service. Raynall Bolling, by then promoted to colonel, was killed while serving in France in 1918. Buried in the Somme American Cemetery, Colonel Bolling is considered officially missing in action. His legacy, however, as the pioneer of military aviation is very real and very apparent today.

The "Lost Battalion" of 1918 tells the tale of another heroic National Guard aviation endeavor. Citizen-soldiers, Federalized under the National Defense Act of 1916, flew to the rescue of 550 members of the 77th Infantry Division when they got separated from their mates in the forests of the Argonne, France. Surrounded and under fire from both the Americans and the Germans, The Battalion commander, Major Whittlesey sent his last carrier pigeon, "Cher Amie", to warn allied troops of their predicament. Planes from the 50th Aero Squadron flew over the Battalion dropping food and supplies until the troops could be safely extracted. After repeated attempts, pilots Lt. Harold Goettler and Kansas National Guardsman, Lt. Erwin Bleckley finally succeeded. Shot down that night, they did not survive the ordeal and were posthumously awarded the Medal of Honor. Such bravery represents the Categorical Imperative by personifying the universal duty to aid comrades even at the risk of losing one's own life. Lt. Erwin Bleckley, a Guardsman and volunteer, repeatedly flew in support of the Lost Battalion in order to ensure their recovery. Surely he, of all airmen that day, represented the universal duty to support one's community through voluntary service.

Another significant contribution made by citizen-soldiers living up to the Enlightenment concept of the Categorical Imperative and its role in the duty to community was reflected by the willingness of northern, urban African Americans to enter the National Guard in service during World War One. The 93rd Division included the 369th Infantry Regiment (15th Regiment – New York National Guard) (Colored). Hundreds of African Americans volunteered for service overseas and made up several infantry regiments. The difficulty of their endeavor was not lost on them for the doctrine of "separate but equal" ensconced in the Supreme Court *Plessy v. Ferguson*, 163 US 537 (1896) decision was still valid law in the United States. Due to the army's embrace of racial segregation, the "colored" troops required separate mess tents, billeting, latrines, leadership, medical facilities, and any other necessary support function. These soldiers really exemplified the ideal of doing one's duty even when one would not personally benefit – especially notable in light of the limited (if any) advancements in civil rights that would emerge in the United States after the War. Because their service presented such logistical challenges under Pershing's regime, the 369th ended up serving most of their combat time with the French Army. As an imperial power in Africa that embraced a doctrine of civilizing its subjects and assimilating them into French culture, the French had no such racial segregation policies. The single most famous soldier to emerge from World War One in the African American corps was Sgt. Henry Johnson. His meritorious service in May, 1918 resulted in the awarding of a Distinguished Service Cross – which, in 2015, was changed to a Medal of Honor.

The African American service in the National Guard during World War One may fairly be viewed as an attempt to further the cause of racial equality and advancement – with little or no sense of higher duty. However, I believe that the African American represented the Categorical Imperative in action for two reasons. First being precisely that the cause of racial equality and advancement could only, at that time in the United States, be advanced through a sense of selfless, non-circumstance based universal fairness and even-handed service. No matter the consequences, an opportunity to serve a higher cause and to do it well-fulfilled intentions to strive toward equal treatment under the law. Additionally where better to attempt that service than under the strict guidelines both required and enforced in an army during wartime? Also note, by assimilating with the French Army, the African American soldiers were able to return to the United States with first-hand experience of equal treatment. But secondly, and more to the point, it can fairly be stated that the African American troops who served in the National Guard during World War One had no realistic hopes of changing conditions in the United States during their lifetimes. Some in the African American community may have felt that service was a fruitless endeavor. And yet, true to the fundamental notion of the Categorical Imperative, the African American men who did volunteer did so anyway – even in light of those reasonably anticipated insurmountable odds. It was a universal voluntary service, fair to the men within their units, and overcoming any threat of being used as a means to an end by controlling their own destinies (at least as far as military service was concerned).

Such examples of grass-roots community support of the national interests put human faces on the Kantian Categorical Imperative. Although these examples of heroic Guardsmen represent their first overseas battles that are not in direct defense of the United States, it is important to note that the need for civic military duty at home endured. Based on the powerful National Defense Act of 1916,

> When the Guard entered into federal service during World War I and was totally absorbed for the first time in its history, leaving no forces on the home front, the National Guard was replaced by the State Guard. The organization of the States Guard in both World Wars I and II is a measure of the vital need for soldiers of the states, and proof that the states could not carry out their business if there was no available force.[40]

Thus, reflecting the Utilitarian need of the states to manage their local order, the citizenry of the many states coincidentally wielded the Kantian Categorical Imperative – realizing that they had a duty to protect the community that was universal, fair, and did not use them as a means to an end. The Citizen-soldiers, when called upon to serve the country in interests beyond their own borders would be supplemented by state guard forces at home that arose *sui generis* and disbanded upon their return.

In a fall 2018 seminar, Major General Don Dunbar, the Adjutant General of Wisconsin and Chairman of the Board of the National Guard Association of the United States, reiterated the concepts and ideas spoken of by General Charles Dick's great-grandson, Charles Tharp. In his civilian capacity, General Dunbar practices law in Wisconsin and is an *aficianado* of the history of the Dick Act of 1903. The National Guard under the Dick Act was a landmark change that provided federal funding to the states and set a common training standard for

---

[40] National Association of Attorneys General, *Legal Issues Concerning the role of the National Guard in Civil Disorders: Staff Report to the Special Committee on Legal Services to Military Forces*, 54.

the National Guard.[41] The Dick Act came as a response to the rapidly changing needs of the United States as it evolved through the mid-19th Century and into the 20th Century. The significance of this groundbreaking legislation should not be underestimated. In just seventy years, by 1973, the United States and a very different National Guard would realize how important the American universal sense of duty, fair treatment, and service would impact its role in foreign wars and the national sentiment towards its military as a whole.

The Industrial Revolution and the turmoil caused by a widely divided economic social structure created new roles for the National Guard – from Governor-ordered strike breakers to international soldiers on the complicated and tumultuous Mexican border. Throughout the upheaval of the Gilded Age and the Progressive Age, the Categorical Imperative remained universal (as it should) regarding service in a volunteer state militia. Such examples of service include the militias of the states and territories during the Plains Indian Wars, the soldiers on the Mexican border, the aviators who simply wanted to fly for the adventure, and the African American troops in World War One who wanted to see the world. The advent of the Dick Act of 1903 provided federal money to the states to support these troops and to ensure that training, benefits, and equipment met minimum standards. And, yet, while the Act provided federal funds, state control of the National Guard stayed the same. Ultimately, the National Guard became a state-based force whose roots could still be traced to the Categorical Imperative – service in response to a sense of higher duty in the defense and protection of community. The Dick Act, because it was based on a financial interaction between the federal government and the states, introduced a Utilitarian philosophy in which one could perfectly validly argue that the cost to benefit ration of the National Guard well out-weighed the standing army.

As I will show in the next chapter, from 1903 onward, most arguments for funding from the federal government would rely on that very Utilitarian proposition. However, the nature of voluntary service in the National Guard remained one of duty to community – particularly as the role of national disaster preparedness expanded. The evidence supporting that proposition lies in the amendment to the Dick Act of 1903, the National Defense Act of 1916 – that expanded the role of the militia and acknowledged both state and federal duty. While in state service, the Militia remained squarely under the control of the Governor, but when federalized, the National Guard of the United States would fall under the rules and regulations of the standing army. Herein lies the strength of the Categorical Imperative in National Guard service in a democratic republic – the duty to one's local community as well as the nation

---

[41] Dunbar lecture, "Legislative History of the National Guard".

both balanced in the right to life, liberty, and the pursuit of happiness. By the time Charles Dick witnessed the mobilization for World War One, his relationship with fellow Ohioan President McKinley was well-vested. The Dick Act had created an environment for the National Guard that would last to this day. Seventy years later, the Total Force Policy would enshrine the pairing of the reserve component (including the federal reserves) to the active duty military in this country. The mistakes made in Vietnam of leaving the Guard behind would never be repeated and the events of 9/11 would cement the relationship further.

In this chapter, the universality of the Categorical Imperative became clear as the United States endures seismic changes both technologically and culturally. Regardless of circumstances or benefits of outcomes, the Militia and its metamorphosis into the National Guard of the United States always relied on the Enlightenment theories upon which the Constitution was founded. With respect for human dignity and the authority granted to the legislatures by the voting population, soldiers continued to serve in the defense of their communities. The next chapter, whose focal figure is General Frank P. Grass, will show how this unchanging duty and its manifestation in the National Guard persisted through the twentieth century and into the current era.

Chapter V

The National Guard and the Post-Modern Era From 1920 to 2020, and Beyond: General Frank P. Grass

I do believe our men and women serving in the National Guard are called to a higher duty. While serving as the Chief of the National Guard Bureau I was fortunate to visit many of our National Guard units, both at home and abroad. I departed these visits energized by these women and men who serve in the National Guard. Their reasons for serving are many but the one attribute that stands out is a calling to "a higher duty" and "a chance to contribute to something larger than themselves.[1]
General Frank P. Grass, Chief, National Guard Bureau, Member, Joint Chiefs of Staff

While the nineteenth century Industrial Revolution transformed the U.S. from a collection of rural and small-town communities into a world economic power, the changes that the U.S. underwent in the twentieth century, rendering it the world's leading superpower, proved perhaps the strongest challenge to the endurance of the Citizen-soldier model of military service. In this chapter, I will discuss the application of Kant's Categorical Imperative across this seismic transition from the Modern to the Post-Modern era. General Frank P. Grass' insightful leadership during this period provides a fitting example of how the Categorical Imperative remains universal and unchanging in a world that keeps moving at breakneck speed.

In 1795, Immanuel Kant wrote his final work, *Toward Perpetual Peace*. He built the monograph upon the Categorical Imperative and designed it to lay out a plan for global harmony. It is small work but arguably supplied the blueprint for the League of Nations and its successor the United Nations. Although Kant did not deny the right of a state to defend itself, the moral law required a code of behavior that was universal, fair, and non-manipulative. The key was that an

---

[1] Frank P. Grass, General (Ret.), Chief, National Guard Bureau, Member, Joint Chiefs of Staff, answers to questionnaire by author, St. Louis, November 16, 2018.

action taken must always be the in use of a human being as an end to itself – never as a means to an end. By which, we infer that a concept of a draft, which involves using men to win a war (as opposed to men themselves pursuing their own life, liberty, and happiness), would be an anathema. In this formulation, one can readily find respect and consideration for human dignity. Kant himself observed,

> Standing armies (*miles perpetuus*) shall in time be abolished altogether. For they incessantly threaten other states with war; they spur states on to outdo one another…and inasmuch as peace, by the costs related to it, finally becomes even more oppressive than a short war, a standing army is itself the cause of an offensive war…. But it is quite different with military exercises undertaken voluntarily and periodically by citizens of a state in order to secure themselves and their own country….[2]

The end of World War One brought a dark, forbidding turn to Western European culture. The brutal reality of trench warfare and mustard gas tamped down the bright, hopeful, horizons of the Industrial Revolution, global expansion, and vast advances in medicine, natural and physical sciences, and improvements of quality of life experienced by many Europeans by the end of the nineteenth century. In so doing, it brought an end to the *Belle Époque*. Romanticism and Modernism gave way to Post-Modern malaise and iconoclasm. In Europe, philosophy began to find itself questioning existence and devolving into a sense of absurdity. Existentialism focused on the rights and needs of the individual – specifically, how individuals could create meaning out of their lives in an absurdly irrational, godless universe. In the United States, having now taken part in a war in a truly global theatre, philosophical theory reexamined William James' pragmatism and demanded an ethics based on objectivity. In particular, the Neo-Pragmatists questioned the ability of normal language to form credible effects on ontology. As philosophy began to respond to the catastrophic nature of World War One, the United States service academies served as useful avenues of information. The military officers of the standing army as well as the reserve components attended these schools as well as civilian universities. By so doing, they were exposed to the changing nature of philosophy's outlook on morality. Although steeped in modern war theory and tactics, the young officers of the day would be well aware of the changes World War One brought to Western Culture as well as to philosophy itself.

---

[2] Kant, *The Cambridge Edition of the Works of Immanuel Kant.*, 318.

The nineteenth century was a very busy one for the United States. The Industrial Revolution made physical and virtual communication faster and more convenient than ever before, politics reeled and adjusted to the growth of corporations managing steel, oil, and electrical production; social responses included the community formations of labor unions, special interest associations, and civil activism; the administrative state evolved from minimal organizations promoting business and unfettered market capitalism to progressive regulatory agencies. By the twentieth century, the military had transformed from a series of small militias governed by the several states to a strong, standing army supported by various forms of militias around the country. Contingencies ranged from serving on the Mexican Border, fighting in the Philippines, and storming San Juan Hill in Cuba. As the citizens of the United States began to move West, so did their thirst for knowledge. Combine that with the increased interest in military service and the rise of service academies came as no surprise. Like the rise of the university system in the eighteenth-century colonies, by the nineteenth century, military academies began to come into their own. Although West Point produced Army officers since the beginning of the Continental Army in 1775; in 1802, the Army officially recognized West Point as a generalized university. In 1845 the Naval Academy took root in Annapolis, Maryland. Although it went through several iterations, the United States Coast Guard Academy was founded in 1876 (and 1890 and again in 1915). As part of the newest service, the Air Force Academy was founded in 1957. Along with these universities, the American military dedicated itself to the pursuit of education through a graduate school system including the Army War College in Carlisle, PA, the Naval War College in Newport, RI, and the Air University, home of Air War College, in Montgomery, AL.

Traditional military education for officers at West Point began as training for civil engineers.[3] The service academy took a sharp turn after the Civil War and began to envision itself as a university to rival its Ivy League neighbors. Such a turn was reflected in military education as a whole and even today in modern literature, the emphasis is being placed on humanities studies.[4] As the nature

---

[3] "A Brief History of West Point", United States Military Academy – West Point, accessed February 13, 2019, https://www.usma.edu/about/history-of-west-point.

[4] As recently as 2010, the Air Force Academy addressed this issue head on. See: Rolf C. Enger, Steven K. Jones and Dana H. Born, "Commitment to Liberal Education at the United States Air Force Academy," *Association of American Colleges & Universities*, Spring 2010, accessed March 4, 2019, https://www.aacu.org/publications-research/periodicals/commitment-liberal-education-united-states-air-force-academy; in 2015, *The Atlantic* published an article discussing the advances in humanities at West Point, see: Jon Marcus, "The Unexpected Schools Championing the Liberal Arts," *The Atlantic*, October

of modern warfare changes, the officer must also be flexible and ready to respond in a variety of circumstances.[5] It is important to point out that the citizen-soldier model encompasses the Army and Air Force ranks from the lowliest enlisted one-striper to the highest four-star general. Service Academies are merely one source of commission in the military and cover all the services as well as the active duty, reserves, and National Guard. In fact, a service Academy is not a traditional source of commissioning for a National Guard officer. It is important, however, for the reader to understand that the military establishment in the United States began to focus more and more on academic learning as the nation and the nature of warfare evolved. What began as a rudimentary educational system in the early colonies grew into a formidable university system sponsored and espoused within the military structure itself. The officers of the day were encouraged to learn and exposed to current educational systems in parallel with the civilian development. Some would argue that the military education system was even superior because it trained young men to be well-rounded – learning humanities, sciences, and military strategy while also studying leadership and stressing sound physical fitness. In fact, one can see the importance of ethics to the West Point curriculum in an 1862 book written by Cadet Benson J. Lossing, *Cadet life at West Point/ By an officer of the United States army. With a descriptive sketch of West Point*. Ethics was a core course at West Point and young Lossing referred to his professor as a "venerable" man who "walked ... majestically into the room".[6]

But returning to the early twentieth century is required to set the stage for the next phase of the citizen-soldier's role in the new world created by the devastation of World War One and the United States' entry into the global stage. With the National Defense Act of 1916, Congress paved the way for National

---

15, 2015, accessed March 4, 2019, https://www.theatlantic.com/education/archive/ 2015/10/the-unexpected-schools-championing-the-liberal-arts/410500/; and as early as 2007, the Department of Defense published an article on well-rounded leadership educated at service academies, specifically mentioning ethics, see: Donna Miles, "Service Academies Retain Principles, Embrace Change to Train Future Leaders," *US Department of Defense, DoD News*, May 24, 2007, accessed March 4, 2019, http://archive. defense.gov/news/newsarticle.aspx?id=46133.

[5] For example see: Joseph Zengerle, "The U.S. military is great on STEM. It should also be great on liberal arts", *The Washington Post Online*, October 3, 2016, accessed February 13, 2019, https://www.washingtonpost.com/posteverything/wp/2016/10/03/the-u-s-milita ry-is-great-on-stem-it-should-also-be-great-on-the-liberal-arts/?utm_term=.f958af170 340.

[6] Benson J. Lossing and George C. Strong, *Cadet life at West Point/By an officer of the United States army. With a descriptive sketch of West Point*, (Boston: T.O.H.P. Burnham, 1862), 76, accessed March 4, 2019, http://digital-library.usma.edu/cdm/ref/collection/ p16919coll10/id/4270.

Guardsmen, volunteers serving their communities in part-time status, to be deployed beyond the borders of their respective states and the nation. By April of 1917, the National Guard Infantry Divisions sent to Europe in support of the United Kingdom and France doubled the size of the regular American Army presence. This powerful number would not go unnoticed by the President and Congress who would later realize the need for manpower outweighed the need for a full-time standing army. By 1940, they again turned to the National Guard to fill the ranks of the active duty as Adolf Hitler's troops marched across Western Europe. The recruitment and popular enlistment of National Guardsmen in 1916 began with the mobilization of existing Militias on the Mexican Border. Once the United States, fed up with German U-boat attacks on the high seas, entered World War One, those troops were moved from the American southwest across the continent and over the Atlantic to the fields of France.

The 59th Pioneer Infantry Regiment of Delaware set a wonderful example of the voluntary and enthusiastic nature of the National Guardsmen in 1917. They had been sent to the Mexican Border to service as engineers, building roads, bridges, and military support camps. When General Pershing returned to Washington, DC to direct the war effort in Europe, the Delaware engineers sped to New York where they knew the troop ships were setting sail. During the initial confusion of the transport, they were able to get berth on a ship by simply taking the place of a unit that did not show up for the launch. By the time the war ended a year later, that same Pioneer Regiment was building roads in the forests of the Meuse-Argonne. The Meuse-Argonne Offensive was the final battle of World War One and the combatants suffered massive casualties. The contested territory included Northeastern France, Belgium, Luxembourg, and Western Germany. In 1917, as the realization sunk in that the United States Army did not have the manpower to fight such a war in Europe, Congress passed the Selective Service Act, 1917. Although this Act required men of a certain age to register for a draft, National Guardsmen remained voluntary. Service to state and country in a militia force remained driven by a universal, fair, and voluntary means of recruitment. A significant number of African American citizens answered the call. By the time the United States formally entered the War, the 369th Infantry Regiment and the 370th Infantry Regiments had formed in New York. Comprised entirely of African American men, they became known as the Harlem Hellfighters. The practical side of their service was complicated by the "separate but equal" social structure still in place in the United States. Of course, the very nature of their segregation from the other troops rendered their service practically unmanageable (hardly equal). The African American troops were led by Caucasian officers and required entirely separate facilities – including dormitories, mess tents, hospital care, and latrines. To overcome these institutionalized hurdles, the 369th and the 370th found themselves in France, fighting with the French Army which welcomed them with open arms. The Harlem Hellfighters ended up seeing a lot of combat and lost more men than any other single American unit in the war. Several of the individual soldiers received recognition for their outstanding service by being awarded Distinguished Service Crosses.[7] Another significant role played by the National Guardsmen who served the higher duty played out in the Meuse-Argonne in the final hours of the War. On November 11, 1918, at 0900 General Pershing called for a drive into the German lines – and the 26th Infantry Division National Guard from Massachusetts answered the call. Over 3000 men were lost that morning. Within two hours, at 1100, representatives of France, England, and Germany signed the Armistice on a train in the Foret de Compiegne – formally ending the "War to End All Wars".

The return of the surviving American soldiers to the United States met with mixed national emotions. The African American troops, expecting to find greater assimilation into the culture, found themselves confronted with the same if not more virulent discrimination. And yet, inroads had been made into the military – an open door for African Americans that would not close again. That door would not swing wide until after World War Two. It is significant to note, that even with the stumbling blocks placed in their way to prevent military service, minority groups in the United States still answered the higher duty to serve in the National Guard of their respective states. The Kantian Enlightenment moral law truly did apply universally, envisioned as a fair duty for all to perform, and did not draw upon personal service as a means to an end but as an end in itself.

World War One had a unique, challenging effect on those participants in both America and Europe. The impact stretched far and wide – in all aspects of society, from economic, to social culture, to industry, to the arts. Philosophy, long determined to be the bellwether of societal mood, began to react strongly to the horrors and frustration of trench warfare. World cultures that had been riding high on the Industrial and Scientific Revolutions, the advancement of sciences, the extravagant wealth of the upper classes, and the development of methods of communication – suddenly tumbled into a morass of despair. "The Lost Generation" of young men who had died in the trenches of France and Germany and would not return home left behind them dumbfounded societies whose members were dismayed at the ability of mankind to be so ruthless and wage such a terrible war upon itself. Thus, philosophy evolved from the enthusiastic and positive Romantic era and the Modern era, into the Post-Modern iconoclasm of the twentieth century. Led by such Existentialists as

---

[7] This service was absolutely above and beyond – so much so that, during his administration, President Obama changed the DSCs to Medals of Honor.

Sartre, de Beauvoir, and Camus, the academic philosophers began to question the purpose of man's existence. Finding frustration and anxiety, they concluded that life was absurd and any pursuit of an ultimate good was fruitless. Ironically, they only had a few years before Europe would find itself falling into yet another World War – this one impossibly worse than the first.

The United States, not immune to the turbulence in Europe, unevenly welcomed its soldiers back to home soil. At first, there was no doubt that the National Guardsmen who served would remain in their units – answering the call of the higher duty as they had since the inception of the nation. However, World War One took its miserable toll on Americans and those who returned suffered the same "shell shock" and desire to return to a normal life that their compatriots in Europe did. The Kantian ideal of a higher duty is just that and is not being argued otherwise – it is an ideal moral law that supersedes circumstances and consequences. That higher duty is not always attained. In post-World War-One America, the returning soldiers left the National Guard in droves. A concerned federal government acted accordingly and developed methods to keep Guardsmen in the service. The demobilization of the regular army and the National Guard was so overwhelming that, as Congress tried to keep men in, the War Department recommended an alternative. In light of the fear of returning to the Uptonian theory of a large standing military, "[John McAuley] Palmer recommended a much smaller regular force…because he viewed the nation's citizen-soldiery…as the bedrock of U.S. land forces, a principle he saw as part of the 'national genius and tradition".[8] Interestingly, he had the support of General Pershing who had originally been doubtful of the talents of the National Guard militiamen.[9]

In 1920, the War Department opened a small office called the Militia Bureau, federally funded, to manage the National Guard at a federal level. Only seventeen years after the Dick Act, Congress was still trying to iron out the role of these volunteer militiamen who answered the call of their local communities and states with reference to a rapidly growing international role to be played by the United States. It is important to note that until 1903, essentially, the Militias had been governed and paid for by the individual states as laid out in the Militia Act of 1792. Such a financial burden became onerous when the Militias found themselves in federal service like the Spanish-American War in 1898 and the Philippines Insurrection of the same year. The Dick Act answered that call by granting federal funds to the states for federal militia service. By 1916, when the National Defense Act then acknowledged the legality of sending militia troops into international theaters, the National Guard could be "Federalized" and

---

[8] Marion and Hoffman, *Forging a Total Force*, 21.
[9] Ibid.

placed under the command and control of the federal government. In some ways, this seems to be reiterating a point already made in this book, but it is critical to the point and bears repetition. By 1916 Federalized National Guardsmen moved from state duty to federal duty. This pathway led to a conundrum in 1918 when the demoralized soldiers from the trenches of Europe returned to the U.S. and wanted to be released from service. During the demobilization, dismayed Governors realized they had no way to re-recruit veterans into their old militia units. By 1933 Congress amended the National Defense Act of 1916 to alter the demobilization status – under this new amendment, when a National Guardsman who joined the state service found himself federalized, upon demobilization, he would automatically revert to state service. The National Defense Act of 1933 created a federal force called the National Guard of the United States (rather than the Nebraska National Guard or a state-specific force). When a state National Guardsman, Federalized into service of the National Guard of the United States, returned from international duty, he would revert back into his State National Guard. (In other words, he would not be released back into the purely civilian population). At that point, he was welcome to renounce his militia membership but had to be proactive in so doing.[10]

The debate around sending National Guardsmen overseas in defense of national interests was settled, and challenges to the status quo would not arise again except in Supreme Court cases that ironed out unique situations like training exercises.[11] It is critical to understand the current literature on the study of the development of the interdependence of the National Guard and the Federal Government at this juncture in the timeline in order to understand the effect of volunteerism on the communities and culture of America as a whole moving forward. Born in turbulence, small, community-based militias adapted to a federal Constitution based on Enlightenment theory and with a Kantian Categorical Imperative motive that wafted overhead. By the nineteenth century, the modern, evolving world began to change the nature of military service once again. No longer were trayned-bands of village men from 16 to 60 years of age meeting on the central green with their muskets and gunpowder for a day of marksmanship practice. When twentieth-century

---

[10] For a beautiful, simple outline of this system from 1792 to 1933, see Major General Dunbar's briefing. "[As of 1933, u]pon being relieved from active duty in the military service of the United States, all individuals and units revert to their status in the National guard of the respective states."

[11] See *Perpich v. DoD,* 496 U.S. 334 (1990) in which National Guardsmen on Title X orders in a training capacity still fall under the purview of the standing Army and must adhere to Army regulations.

militiamen answered the call to serve that duty sent them far afield and into a much more threatening environment of mustard gas, trench foot, and mortar fire.

Even at home, the disaster and civil disorder melees were changing hue. What began in the nineteenth century as union strike busting became a national struggle to manage the new generation of freed African Americans who were seeking their civil rights in a world of Jim Crow and oppression. In 1921, the race riot in Tulsa, Oklahoma sent a jolt of horror through the local community. Limited news reports in national coverage kept the incident away from widespread public knowledge but it was a clear harbinger of things to come. Over a couple of early summer days, African American World War one veterans, armed from the National Guard Armory, attempted to assist the Tulsa police force as they protected a young African American man accused of molesting a white elevator operator from what seemed to be a gathering white lynch mob. In response, white residents armed themselves. The fear and hysteria escalated drawing African Americans and Caucasians in from neighboring towns. By the end of the first day, the Oklahoma National Guard arrived and declared martial law. "The Black district [of Tulsa], a mile square, was burned down, and between 85 and 150 died. Martial law was proclaimed and the guard placed the Black survivors in detention camps for their own safety".[12] Interestingly, charges against the boy were dropped and he was released the following morning. The rest of the nation was by no means immune to race riots and as early as 1919, Washington DC, Chicago, IL, Charleston, SC, Knoxville, TN, and Omaha, NE had suffered such violence. These riots – as terrible and disruptive as they may have been – demonstrated the duality of the National Guard's role in its continued history as a military service both at home and abroad. Soldiers freshly returned from the trenches of Europe were confronted with domestic civil disputes that kept them both armed and in uniform. Despite the fact that they had returned home to confront violence similar to that they had seen in the trenches of Europe and despite their own political and social sentiments, the guardsmen had to draw upon the Categorical Imperative to protect the public – regardless of circumstances and possible outcome. The Kantian Categorical Imperative was tested and proven to be universal in service to one's community.

The domestic support provided by the National Guard during the civil disorder of the years between World Wars One and Two enabled governors to

---

[12] National Association of Attorneys General, *Legal Issues Concerning the role of the National Guard in Civil Disorders: Staff Report to the Special Committee on Legal Services to Military Forces*, 55, quoting *Kinsella v. Singleton*, 361 U.S. 234 (1961); *Grisham v. Hagan*, 361 U.S. 278 (1961); *McElray v. Guagiliardo*, 361 U.S. 281 (1961).

"flex their muscles" as commanders in chief of their militias on home turf and also sent the 1878 law of *Posse Comitatus* through the courts. Consistently upheld, *Posse Comitatus* continued to enforce the separation of a domestic military force and the police powers of a local constabulary – legally, those lines were never to blur. In practice, however, they certainly did. The Kantian Categorical Imperative, by definition universal, applied to the police as well who were supposed to protect the citizens of their communities. In light of the National Guard's performance in Europe, however, the Congress and Executive Branch of the Federal Government began to realize how important the reserve component was to increased manpower on the global front. In 1920 and in 1933, Congress acted to clarify the role of the National Guard in the broader scope and to structure the force to be more efficient as the primary reserve of the Army. Some have called the years between the wars the National Guard's "struggle to survive". The point they make is that the National Guard's role was finally being narrowly defined by law and there was a good chance it would be subsumed into the standing army and absorbed by the federal reserve force, which had developed in parallel. The profound role played by the militia in the United States since the nation's inception prevented that from happening. The National Defense Act of 1920 created a Militia Bureau, staffed by standing army officers and nestled in an office within the War Department. "[C]ontrol of the Militia Bureau ... [was taken] away from the regular Army and required that a National Guard major general serve as the bureau chief. The new chief also reported to an assistant secretary of war, not the Army chief of staff".[13] The significance of this change is manifold – the citizen-soldiers of the United States were now represented in the War Department by one of their own, a leader who had risen to Adjutant General status within the Militia system, and answered directly to the War Department – not as a subservient member of the standing Army. The interests and goals of the National Guard would be less likely thwarted by the standing army that alternatively saw the Guard as a help and a hindrance.

Major General John McAuley Palmer, who was a powerhouse during this period of Guard development, espoused a new form of recruitment for the National Guard – Universal Military Training (UMT). The UMT concept hovered around mandatory training for soldiers followed by voluntary, part-time service in their state and community reserve components.[14] Between the wars, the National Guard saw its own best interest advanced by adhering to the

---

[13] Marion and Hoffman, *Forging a Total Force*, 22.

[14] Note, in this case, "soldiers" referred to male citizens. Interestingly, those disqualified for medical reasons were almost all suffering from dental maladies. Recruitment of dentists was always a priority.

Dick Act's mandate to parallel the standing Army in training, equipment supply, and compensation. This interest was entirely in the pursuit of maintaining the National Guard as the standing army's primary reserve force. UMT first came to the attention of the National Guard leadership before World War One and focused on domestic "preparedness". Supported by President Roosevelt, the idea gained momentum. After National Guard soldiers returned from Europe, however, two competing factions arose. Those who followed the old Uptonian theory of a large standing army of trained volunteers conflicted with those who followed Palmer's concept of a small standing army with citizen-soldier components throughout the nation, trained for activation when needed. While UMT could fit into either format, it was not popular with Palmerians. The primary reticence was a reluctance to agree to anything that looked like a draft.[15] UMT was controversial but set the stage for the National Guard Association of the United States, the civilian organization created after the Civil War during post-Reconstruction, to look after the citizen-soldier. By 1933, the citizen-soldier model in the United States had taken some strong hits – troops returning from the trenches of Europe were no longer interested in serving in capacity that had been advertised as supporting their local communities but ended up in a Belgian hellhole. Because the National Defense Act of 1916 provided no means to keep soldiers in the National Guard once they had been placed on federal duty overseas, the National Guard at home had begun to hemorrhage soldiers. This blood-letting came to the attention of Congress mainly after the War as the shell-shocked soldiers began to return. Soured on military service, Guardsmen shed their uniforms as their federal service orders came to a close. Over time, and in response to this loss, Congress passed the National Defense Act of 1933 which specifically placed redeployed National Guardsmen back into their original status as citizen-soldiers. Once they returned, they would then have to proactively resign their enlistments or commissions in order to leave the Guard. This point is quite significant because it marked the beginning of reliance by the upper echelons of the military command on the Utilitarian argument for maintaining manpower numbers in the local militias. The argument, rather than the "higher duty" put forth by the Categorical Imperative, used Utilitarian cost/benefit analysis to justify this redeployment and – because it was based in irrefutable mathematics and in the language of the country's exigent manpower needs – usually won the day.

The National Guard continued to demonstrate the Categorical Imperative in action – a tribute to the Enlightenment theory upon which the nation and the

---

[15] See Doubler, Hill, and Marion and Hoffman in general on the subject. Nothing is ever clearly defined because UMT died on the vine. The threat of mandatory training, however, did not sit well with Guard leadership.

Constitution was based – when the economic world fell apart in October of 1929. The Great Depression hit the United States and, practically overnight, hundreds of thousands of Americans lost their savings. All over the country, National Guard armories opened up to support the local communities. Where drilling National Guardsmen had before eaten and slept during their monthly weekend service, now there were daily soup kitchens and complete dormitories to feed and house those citizens left destitute by the Depression. By 1933 and in response to the effects of the Depression, President Franklin D. Roosevelt and the Congress passed a series of acts to put Americans to work on government projects and to fund private projects with federal money. The National Guard found itself integrally involved in the Civilian Conservation Corps (CCC) which was managed by General George C. Marshall. The CCC consisted of camps throughout the country where young men trained and maintained an almost military lifestyle. During his time directing the CCC, Marshall spent several months training the Illinois Army National Guard. According to Forrest C. Pogue, author of a multi-volume biography of the General, Marshall found the CCC and the National Guard a source of his faith in the concept of a Citizen-soldier army.[16] The idea of serving the community through the National Guard and through the CCC perfectly encapsulated the Categorical Imperative in action – service was universally accepted behavior, viewed as fair, and directly aided the community using no man as a means to an end.

On the international stage, in September, 1939, German Chancellor Adolph Hitler invaded Poland – igniting a second World War and rendering the First World War moniker "the War to end all wars" moot. Germany swept through Europe and in June of 1940, France fell. By September, 1940, President Roosevelt and the Congress mobilized the National Guard of the United States (recall that the NDA of 1933 created that entity of federalized militia soldiers). Grateful for work and pay, the citizen-soldiers of the many states deployed within the continental United States to take part in The Great Maneuvers. These "games" were designed to get the National Guard and the standing army prepared should the Congress declare war and join the Allies in the fight against Nazi Germany in Europe. Once again, the Categorical Imperative came into play as the voluntary service (certainly encouraged by the needs created during the Depression) supported the needs of the community. Soldiers, who before depending on their own wits and the programs set up by FDR's New Deal, now benefited from the Great Maneuvers. In turn, the communities rose to the call

---

[16] Jeffery, "Marshall and the Civilian Conservation Corps," George C. Marshall Foundation, March 3, 2017, accessed February 15, 2019, https://www.marshallfoundation.org/blog/marshall-civilian-conservation-corps/.

and supported their transplanted troops. In all, by September 1940, some 300,000 National Guardsmen were on the move, training for a potential deployment. The structure of the National Guard underwent one of its most substantial changes when it went from the traditional rectangular structure within Divisions to a three-part system called "triangularization".

> Earlier in 1941, the Army had created a "triangular division" based on the employment of three infantry regiments, and active duty divisions converted to the new design. Stripped of all unnecessary combat and support units, the smaller triangular division was designed for agility and responsiveness on the fluid battlefields of mechanized warfare. After Pearl Harbor, the Army directed the Guard divisions to convert from the square to the triangular configuration.[17]

In so doing, the National Guard mirrored its peer, the regular Army and took yet another critical step toward what would become the Total Force Policy – building on the legacy started by General Charles Dick in 1903. Harkening back to the original Enlightenment roots of the citizen-soldier, the National Guard employed its willing volunteers developing primary strategic reserve for the full time standing army. Based on the voluntary nature of the service, the Guardsmen entering a strategic reserve, while appearing to be a means to an end, were still performing their duty as community protectors. The now-deployable National Guard never lost its role as the primary resource for the protection of the community when confronted with civil disorder or natural disaster. Additionally, the soldier knew through daily life that Democracy was worth the sacrifice on an international scale. The leadership, relying on Utilitarian arguments, approved – while the typical National Guardsman adapted his service to support the career soldiers.

Then, on December 7, 1941, the Japanese invaded Pearl Harbor, Hawaii, and the American entrance into World War Two became inevitable. Almost immediately, the National Guard launched nine divisions to each theater, both in Europe and Asia. All eighteen divisions presented the largest mobilization of the National Guard in its history. As in World War One, the National Guard comprised fully half of the Army readiness and presence. The track in the Pacific followed by the National Guard led soldiers through the island-hopping scheme of General Douglas MacArthur. By May of 1942, the 23d Division

---

[17] Doubler, *Civilian in Peace, Soldier in War*, 203.

"Americal"[18] entered the first theater of combat at Guadalcanal. National Guardsmen saw action in all battles and suffered through unspeakable hardships including the Bataan Death March with their regular army peers. A man who would later become the Adjutant General of the National Guard of Massachusetts, Charles Sweeney, was the primary pilot of a B-29 called Bockscar – the sister aircraft to the Enola Gay. Under Sweeney's command, the atomic bomb, "Fat Man", decimated Nagasaki on August 9, 1945.

The trail of combat for the National Guard in Europe began in the United Kingdom for additional training and then to North Africa. In North Africa, the 34th Infantry Division met with General George Patton and 3rd Army. Together, they defeated the Axis in Tunisia and fought up the boot of Italy. Met from the East and the North by the 45th Infantry Division, the National Guard continued its combat into central Europe. June 6th, 1944, marked the date of the largest amphibious invasion in the history of the military of the United States. Led by General Dwight D. Eisenhower, the American forces landed on the beaches of Normandy early in the morning and in terrible weather. 1st Army and the 29th Infantry Division (DC, MD, VA) of the National Guard led the way. In particular, the 116th Infantry Regiment took out an .88 mm gun on the west side of Omaha Beach while 1st Army took out the sister gun to the east – opening the Vierville-sur-Mer draw and allowing the soldiers access to the French countryside. Occupied since 1940, the French were overwhelmed with relief as the allied soldiers stormed into their villages.[19] By this time, the Army Air Corps was in full flight and within days began to flatten German outposts in the northern regions of France as the Army marched toward Paris and onward. The end of the war was now seen as possible – if not probable. It would be another eleven months before Adolph Hitler committed suicide in a bunker and the Germans once again surrendered to Allied forces. The 28th Infantry Division of the Pennsylvania National Guard celebrated the liberation of Paris in August of 1944 while the 45th Infantry Division (OK, NM, CO, AZ) marched toward the front lines and into Germany proper. By April of 1945, near the end of the war, members of the 45th Infantry Division and the 30th Infantry Division "Old Hickory" (TN, SC, NC) had critical roles in the liberation of the Munich concentration camp in Dachau. Led by Lt. Col Felix Sparks of the 45th, National Guard soldiers opened the gates of Dachau and were the first to witness the real

---

[18] The Americal Division was the only division ever to be formed outside of the continental United States and was so named because it consisted of American National Guardsmen and natives of the island of New Caledonia.

[19] The author has made several trips to the Vierville draw (an opening of dunes) and without question, the locals all say their parents and grandparents met the incoming troops with a sense of relief at the liberation.

horror of the Holocaust. The role of the National Guard in the two theatres of World War Two cannot be overstated.

During the period of time that the vast majority of the National Guard was overseas in Europe and the Pacific theater, Roosevelt and Congress were calculating ways to keep Guardsmen involved in the Army and the fledgling Army Air Corps. General Palmer stressed the importance of a Universal Military Training (UMT) program while the National Guard Association of the United States, led by General Ellard A. Walsh, pushed back. The traditional role of the National Guard as a citizen-soldier force ran deeply in the American culture and psyche – a long-term mandatory training program described by Palmer ran against that tide. Although Palmer argued against UMT, he accepted that it might be necessary to maintain the Guard's relationship with the standing army. However, Walsh fought to maintain relevance for the National Guard, which constantly felt under pressure from Congress to coalesce the federal reserves and the Guard into a single reserve force. Walsh held firm – if any reserve component would come out on top, it would be the National Guard. He was willing to compromise with Palmer and agreed to UMT if Palmer would concur that the Dick Act of 1903 held sway, stating unequivocally that the National Guard remained the primary reserve force for the standing army. But Walsh was not satisfied yet – he went on to argue that the concept of an Air Force, floating around the War Department, should have a parallel in the National Guard. By 1946, the 120th Observation Squadron, Colorado Army National Guard, returned to the United States and was told not to disband. Within months they were designated members of the Colorado Air National Guard. Not until September 1947 would Congress officially announce the formation of a separate military organization known simply as the United States Air Force. By the end of World War Two, the National Guard was integrally involved in both theatres. Guardsmen had witnessed both the horrors of nuclear warfare and of the Holocaust. Citizen-soldiers met with systematic genocide alongside their active duty peers on both fronts of the Second World War. For the National Guard and the understanding of the higher duty to serve, there was no turning back from the understanding that they were now a part of man's willingness and ability to annihilate entire races. The impact of the nuclear destruction ushering in the atomic age and of the Holocaust cannot be overstated – and the United States National Guard was witness to both.

At this juncture, it is critical to discuss how the events of World War Two affected the philosophers of Western Europe. The pogroms of the War and the dawning realization of the Holocaust had a profound impact on prevailing senses of man's existence. The absolute destructive nature of the atomic bombs dropped on Nagasaki and Hiroshima – demonstrating the ability of mankind to both wonder at quantum mechanics as well as realize how fully we could destroy ourselves – was no less significant than the systemic destruction wrought by the Holocaust. During the war, many philosophers in Germany and occupied France fled when and where they could. Western Europe, reeling from the devastation and demoralization of World War One, braced itself for recovery after World War Two. Those academics fortunate enough to escape Hitler's thorough ethnic cleansing, migrated beyond the continent – many ending up in New York. Of those philosophers, one of the most influential, Hannah Arendt (1906-1975) spent her time teaching at the City University of New York, where she studied the nature of totalitarianism. Arguably, a series of articles written for the *New Yorker* magazine in 1961 are her most famous work. Searching for war criminals, the Israelis found Otto Adolf Eichmann (1906-1962) in Argentina and brought him back to stand trial. Hannah Arendt witnessed the entire trial on behalf of the magazine. Her takeaway was that evil is truly banal – there is a disengagement of thought from action. For Arendt, the evil of the Holocaust was personified by Eichmann's inability to think critically. Arendt's insight into evil impressed the philosophical community in part because of her life leading up to that moment. Born in Germany, Arendt was a student and protégé of Martin Heidegger (1889-1976). There can be little doubt that Heidegger was a proper Nazi throughout his life – he never left Germany, actively maintained a membership in the Nazi Party, and even went so far as to wear his party pin routinely on his lapel. Heidegger's principal focus was on mankind's role in language and existence. He profoundly influenced the movement of hermeneutics that would flourish in the twentieth century and beyond. When Arendt, a Jew, fled Germany for France and ultimately New York, Heidegger remained behind. Another vitally important philosopher, whose life was relatively short, was Simone Weil (1909-1943). A French Jew, she migrated to London where she stayed until the war was almost over – dying at only 34 years of age. Influenced by the works of Plato, her philosophy touched on both Kant's *Toward a Perpetual Peace* and Wilson's brilliant concepts behind the League of Nations. Based on Kant's Categorical Imperative as well as the ideas of free will, Weil stressed that a government's authority in regulating society arise from the individual as a desire to serve rather than from some form of authoritarian government requiring service. As with the Enlightenment idea "of the people, by the people, and for the people" Weil wrote that the authority to grant service to one's community must come from the individual. This theory builds on earlier ideas, as described in this book, in which Enlightenment theory in the eighteenth century was then applied to the concept of representative government. The individual was granted the right to pursue his own life, liberty, and happiness as well as to ensure the representative form of government acted on the wishes of the governed.

By the end of World War Two, Western Europe was again demolished – but this time, there now hung a shroud of the Holocaust and the stunningly horrific knowledge of the power of the atomic bomb. Philosophy responded in kind – moving from the Modern to the Post Modern. Post-Modern philosophy was iconoclastic, despairing, and fatalistic. Philosophers honed in on existential questions as well as the futility and absurdity of life in general. The United States was not immune. And, yet, true to the Kantian concept of the Categorical Imperative – that higher duty remained stubbornly unchanging as applied to the National Guard. 300,000 soldiers began returning to the United States and, thanks to the National Defense Act of 1933, returning to state status in their old home units. Service to their communities remained universal, fair, and un-manipulative. Into Post-War America, the National Guard found itself one again in a fight for its existence – not in spite of its performance in the war but because of it. The United States and, even begrudgingly, the standing army realized they needed the manpower provided by the National Guard. It was now that the federal government began a push to demand that guardsmen serve in a UMT program. Not only did the federal government recognize the need for an Army National Guard – they opened up an Air National Guard at almost the same time they created the United States Air Force. After President Franklin Roosevelt's death, President Truman led the Executive Branch in a demobilization that would focus on training and readiness – a return to the citizen-soldier model and a move away from the standing full-time army.

Looking at the Congressional record, Utilitarianism still provided the easiest, clearest, and preferable basis for arguing that the Citizen-soldier model was the best for the United States military. Focused on cost/benefit analysis and consequence-driven, Utilitarianism provided a straightforward method of analysis that would always bolster the argument for the National Guard. A part-time reserve force, the Guard was almost always cheaper to maintain and could promise the "bang for the buck". The compromise for readiness, though, meant that the Guard had to agree to maintain a certain threshold of readiness to meet the basic balance in the Utilitarian calculation. The National Guard Association of the United States, the civilian lobbying organization established in 1878, began negotiating with Congress and, its president, Ellard A. Walsh, agreed to support UMT only if Congress would agree to give Guardsmen better retention and retirement benefits. Along with those demands, Walsh wanted a restatement of the National Guard as the primary reserve force of the smaller standing army as well as a partner to the fledgling Air Force.

Although Congress never implemented UMT, this negotiation set important twentieth-century precedents for the relationship between the National Guard and the federal government. NGAUS became a loud, powerful voice on Capitol Hill (and remains so to this day) and one Congress heeded. NGAUS engaged in a pitched battle to defeat UMT and its very idea while negotiating for better benefits for Guardsmen, and most importantly, NGAUS' evident power began to focus the Guard's attention on domestic issues like family, community, and state.[20] By the 1960s, and the rise of the threat of Communism, the National Guard suited the new military readiness posture known as "Flexible Response". Secretary of Defense McNamara sought a middle-ground between polar responses to mutually assured destruction which loomed in the wake of the nuclear threat. Flexibility afforded by the citizen-soldier who seamlessly moved back and forth from community to infantry answered that call. As for the rise of Communism and the effect it had on the United States at community level, fear of the USSR overwhelming democracy was very real. During the 1950s, National Guard enrollment remained steady – certainly in light of NGAUS' gains in benefits and retirement funding. The first hint that the Domino Theory (or the separate but equally compelling theory of Containment) was valid came 1950 when North Korea (aided by China and the USSR) invaded South Korea (aided by the US). President Truman federalized the National Guard and immediately mobilized the 28th ID (PA) and the 43rd ID (RI, VT, CT) to Europe and the 40th ID (CA) and the 45th ID (OK) to Japan. By 1951 fully 33% of the entire National Guard had boots on the ground in Korea. Anecdotally, Major Sam Crooks, a volunteer in the Rhode Island Guard, was already in the country when he found himself caught up in the War. In 1948, the Rhode Island Army National Guard sent him to run a textile factory near Seoul. When the war ended, he quietly returned home and resumed his civilian life as a wire-cutter. He remained in the Guard and retired as a Colonel.

By the 1960s, with the demobilization from World War Two and the Korean War, the American military had dwindled to a shadow of its former self. Subtly, between the 1950s' "Red Scare" and the 1960s, the federal government began a slow buildup of US advisors and troops in Southeast Asia. In response to the perceived spread of Communism, the Kennedy Administration began to send advisors to Vietnam and the surrounding countries. By the time of Kennedy's assassination in 1963, his successor Lyndon B. Johnson realized that he would not be able to support a full-fledged war in Vietnam without an element of subterfuge from the American people. To that end, he refused to send the

---

[20] UMT presented a real threat to the volunteer nature of the National Guard. Although batted around for decades, UMT remained ill-defined. What was clear was that it represented a form of military commitment. The Guard leadership maintained a negative view of coerced service for several reasons. Not least of these reasons was the amount of time it would remove the citizen from his civilian life. In a briefing written by General Walsh for NGAUS, he stressed the loss incurred by employers and families by too long a commitment. For example, he specifically suggested that the training period be over the summer to avoid academic conflicts. National Guard Association of the United States Brief on Universal Military Training, 1945, Box 2, Folder 2, Ellard M. Walsh Papers, National Guard Memorial Museum, Library, and Archives, Washington, D.C.

National Guard – in fact, the long, complicated list of deferment options specifically included National Guard service. In other words, if you were in the National Guard, you would be exempt from going to Vietnam. In her book Drift, Rachel Maddow writes very effectively about how this decision diminished the role of the National Guard in the eyes of the local communities.

> The agonized president [Johnson] was trying to thread a new and difficult needle: taking the nation's armed forces to war without taking the nation as a whole to war. And central to that effort was one crucial decision. Against the advice of his secretary of defense [McNamara] and the Joint Chiefs of Staff, over the outright objection of the Chief of Staff of the US Army, Johns simply refused to call up the modern parallel to those old Jeffersonian state militias, all those men living in our neighborhoods: the US Army Reserve and the National Guard.[21]

Although it would seem to appeal to those young men wanting to avoid a draft, the mood of the country was against anyone in a uniform. In lieu of sending the full Army – both standing and reserve component – LBJ chose to institute an unpopular draft. The deferments that were codified by Congress to avoid this draft were so varied (including National Guard service) that the bulk of draftees ended up being the most socially vulnerable young men America could muster.

It has been mentioned before that the Kantian Categorical Imperative is an ideal – and by virtue of being an ideal, it may be desirable but not always obtained. The response to the Vietnam War and recruitment is a good example of the American population turning away from the Categorical Imperative and abstaining from supporting their communities. In particular, the Categorical Imperative requires fairness in the application of the act – the draft and the method of its use in practice was decidedly unfair – randomly calling up those unable to qualify for deferments or legally to avoid mandatory service. The tradition, so long held in the democratic republic, failed to appeal. In part, this repudiation of service may be ascribed to President Nixon's 1969 institution of a formal draft that based enlistment on a mandatory lottery system – the fateful "luck of the draw" was not only distasteful but, instituted by the federal government, smacked broadly of arbitrary coercion of the ordinary citizen into military service. The popular backlash may be viewed as a resounding statement by the population against the war in Vietnam. While the unpopularity and unwinnability of the war may have been the driving force

---

[21] Rachel Maddow, *Drift* (New York: Crown Publishers, 2012), 16.

behind the hatred of the draft, the idea of forced service imposed upon the citizenry of a democratic republic predictably did not sit well.

Such a back-turning could also be explained by the Executive Branch's intentional decision to hold the National Guard back from the War to avoid the appearance of committing a full-fledged war in Southeast Asia. Less a loss of the Categorical Imperative at work in American society at the lowest levels, this corruption of the moral law could be fairly viewed as artificially imposed from above. An important observation may be made here: The most significant time in the history of the United States that the Categorical Imperative, as applied to the National Guard, was ignored or usurped was one in which this breach came from authority from above, not the individual. It is vitally important to realize that the lack of adherence to the Categorical Imperative came, not from the citizenry exhibiting any lack of a will to serve, but to the citizenry chafing under the demand made upon them by authority from the highest levels of government. As demonstrated in this book, the idea of service to the community grew from the Enlightenment theory that authority springs from the governed to the government, not the reverse. The Categorical Imperative fundamentally acts on free will and the rights of the individual to act in pursuit of the universally fair and unmanipulative force of national service. In the case of the LBJ era, a corruption of the Categorical Imperative was driven from the top down and the Imperative was effectively smothered. To be fair, the flame was not entirely extinguished and some 3,000 Army and Air National Guardsmen did serve in Vietnam, some with great distinction.[22]

The advent of protests against an unpopular war and the blossoming Civil Rights Movement in the United States opens up another opportunity to apply the Categorical Imperative to the citizen-soldier concept in a democratic republic. A critical facet to National Guard service entered into the spotlight during the 1960s and 1970s. For the first time, the National Guard's mission spread across two frontiers. The National Guard was engaged in Vietnam and the struggle of balancing restrictions at home versus service overseas at the same time the nation was confronted with possibly the most divisive cultural upheaval since the Civil War. Beginning in the Southern states in the 1950s, the Civil Rights Movement represented African Americans as they strove to be seen as equal citizens of the United States. Their peaceful resistance was met by violence at almost every turn. The South was still held in the sway of old Jim Crow laws and white supremacist leaders while many in the North saw the African Americans as interlopers who threatened jobs, property value, and their own freedoms. For the first time, though, the National Guard had a not

---

[22] However, it must be pointed out that the famous Mai Lai Massacre was perpetrated by Lt. William Calley, Platoon Leader, C Company – a member of the Americal Division.

insignificant combat mission overseas as well as a domestic civil disorder mission at home. This two-fold, complicated change in their traditional structure would change the nature of the National Guard forever. But, as demonstrated throughout this book, the Kantian Categorical Imperative – being universal in nature – did not change. Americans answered the call of a higher duty and, in fact, many draftees and volunteers alike served in Vietnam believing in that duty. One could argue that the National Guard service in Vietnam did represent the Categorical Imperative's universality in that Guardsmen were still willing to serve even in the face of unpopularity – particularly when it came to defending and supporting their local communities.

While some National Guardsmen were, in fact, deployed to Vietnam, most remained stateside. By the early 1960s, the American culture underwent a dramatic upheaval in response to the landmark case, *Brown v. Board of Education*, 347 US 483 (1954) which overturned the "separate but equal" decision in *Plessy v. Ferguson*, 163 US 537 (1896). By virtue of the 14th Amendment, which applies federal law to the states, U.S. public schools were opened to black students in equal measure to white students. By 1964, the federal government passed the Civil Rights Act which, applying to the states, required the country's institutions, from schools and hospitals to movie theatres and restaurants, to desegregate.[23] Those communities in which segregation was entrenched responded loudly and violently. Initially, the Governors of those states called in their National Guard troops to return order. Most famously, Governor George Wallace of Alabama, in 1963, used the National Guard in state status to attempt to stop the integration of the University of Alabama. President John F. Kennedy, using his executive order powers, federalized the Guard and ordered them to remove the governor from the "schoolhouse door".[24] National Guard service, in this situation, was additionally complicated by the disaffection of military service in general by the American people. As anger and frustration mounted against the war in Vietnam, those wearing uniforms – whether in service to help the community avoid violence and destruction or in service overseas – were viewed by the public with consternation and disapproval. Because the National Guard had been left in the United States intentionally under the Johnson Administration

---

[23] The Civil Rights Act of 1964 was followed quickly by the Voting Rights Act of 1965 and the Fair Housing Act of 1968.

[24] The "schoolhouse door" became an apocryphal term coined by Governor George Wallace in his political rhetoric – so instantly recognizable that E. Culpepper Clark titled his account, *The Schoolhouse Door: Segregation's Last Stand at the University of Alabama.*

and was, therefore present to manage the civil disorder of the 1960s, its members bore the brunt of society's fury.

By April, 1968, the simmering anger in the U.S. boiled over when Dr. Martin Luther King, Jr. was assassinated in Memphis, TN. Wild and violent race riots broke out across the country – particularly in Watts, CA; Detroit, MI; Washington, D.C.; Newark, NJ; and Philadelphia, PA to name a few cities. National Guardsmen were called in to quash the disorder. The Staff Report to the Special Committee on Legal Services to Military Forces, written by the National Association of Attorneys General in December of 1973 summarizes the use of National Guardsmen in civil disorder in a single chapter. The report was generated as a response to increased public questioning of the role the Guard and the United States military was permitted by law to play in civil disorder along with public life in general. It states,

> The National Guard has been used literally thousands of times to meet civil disorders and natural emergencies. Regular United States Army troops have also been used in domestic civil disorders, although such use is rare. There have also been instances, both in the early days of the Republic and in recent times, when the President federalized the National Guard, or sent in the regular Army, or used both forces in civil disorder situations.[25]

Most of what the Attorneys General go on to outline has already been discussed previously, and at length, in this book. Of course, the fundamental of this authorization is in the preamble of the Constitution, that the purpose of the government (federal and state) is to "ensure domestic tranquility".[26] Additionally, art. I, sec. 8 gives Congress the power to "call forth" and is known, commonly, as the Militia Clause. In the history of the National Guard – the Categorical Imperative comes most into play when the Guard is supporting and protecting its local community. Briefly, governors used the Guard to quell insurrections over the history of the U.S. primarily as the Guard began to form a cohesive force in the mid-19th Century. These strikes and rebellions have been hashed over in detail in earlier chapters but the civil disorder of the 1960s brought with it the additional complication of the Guard's dual role – both

---

[25] National Association of Attorneys General, *Legal Issues Concerning the role of the National Guard in Civil Disorders: Staff Report to the Special Committee on Legal Services to Military Forces*, 44. They write a good summary of the history of the Guard in civil disorders pages 51-6. These examples of community service are significant because they remain true to the Categorical Imperative's action in supporting the safety of the local community.

[26] US Constitution, preamble.

domestically and internationally. The beauty of the Categorical Imperative in light of these circumstances, though, is that is it universal. Guardsmen served the community, state, and nation to ensure their rights to life, liberty, and the pursuit of happiness would not be infringed upon – whether in their home towns or in Vietnam (they were doing so on the then-accepted domino theory that, if one country fell, it would only be a matter of time before the Communists were in the local bakery.)

Throughout the difficult and complex era of the 1950s, 1960s, and 1970s, the structure of the National Guard and the Department of Defense underwent a theoretical sea change. By that I mean that the Department of Defense began to look more broadly and more expansively at the value the National Guard presented to the domestic and international peace efforts. Force analysis began in the 1950s and continued through the 1960s. In 1970 Secretary of Defense Melvin Laird, supported by Alabama Air National Guardsman, Brigadier General Theodore C. Marrs, proposed a "Total Force Concept". Laird's and Marr's concept, in practice, applied the theory behind the Dick Act of 1903 by completely integrating the part-time forces into the active duty. When called to war, the standing army and air force would immediately rise to the occasion with manpower levels augmented as needed by the reserve component. In theory, the active duty would be "lean and mean" while the citizen-soldier force would join them seamlessly when and if needed.[27] The idea began to percolate through the services, finding a positive response. Having learned a valuable lesson in Vietnam, by 1973, the Chief of Staff of the Army stated "We will never go back to war without the Guard and Reserves".[28] In that statement, General Abrams articulated the need for a Total Force – which would become known as the Abrams Doctrine. And, with this statement, General Abrams ushered in the era of the Total Force Policy which we live under today. In the early 1970s, General Abrams oversaw the "roundout" brigades that reorganized the standing army in order to absorb parts of the Guard and Reserves in time of need. The army would be thinned, cut to its bones with reductions in both manpower and equipment. When needed, then, the Guard would be called upon to "roundout" the army with additional manpower and equipment. Roundout "integrated designated Guard … units into regular brigades or divisions to bring them to full strength upon mobilization".[29] These changes in

---

[27] John T. Correll, "Origins of the Total Force," *Air Force Magazine*, February, 2011, accessed March 7, 2019, http://www.airforcemag.com/MagazineArchive/Pages/2011/February%202011/0211force.aspx.
[28] Lewis Sorely, "Creighton Abrams and Active-Reserve Integration in Wartime", US Army War College Quarterly, *Parameters*, Summer, 1991, 45.
[29] Marion and Hoffman, *Forging a Total Force*, 58.

the role of the National Guard in relation to the standing army also helped to realize the goal set by General Dick in 1903 – that the National Guard become the primary reserve force of the active duty. The 70-year legislative evolution from 1903 to 1973, when the Total Force Policy was signed into effect by Secretary of Defense Schlesinger, also went a step farther than General Dick's original conceptualization by priming the National Guard not only to be a primary reserve force but to also be prepared to lead the way – it anticipated the transition of the Guard from a strategic reserve to an operational force, riding on the tip of the spear with its fulltime counterparts.[30]

By the end of the Vietnam War in 1973, the U.S. transitioned back to an all-volunteer force. Abrams' great insight was to see that the cultural fabric of the United States, from 1636 moving forward, demanded that military service be voluntary and driven with respect for the Enlightenment "pursuit of life, liberty, and happiness". While meeting the needs of the Federal government protecting the interests of the United States both foreign and domestic, the root of the American military must be nurtured at the local level. And, there was no better place to start than the state level National Guard. Recall that most National Guardsmen drilled at their local armories for years, some for generations. Unless performing the vestiges of UMT, "summer two-week drill", Guardsmen rarely had call to leave their local communities. During the 1970s and '80s, mainly an era of peace for the United States, the Congress and Joint Chiefs of Staff began to look inwards – to reevaluate the needs of the Army and the Air Force based on their substantial reserve forces. The Categorical Imperative, universal and fair, continued to articulate itself in the volunteer force and the locally based, community-oriented National Guard. In peacetime, the Guard had the opportunity to focus on its personnel as well as the support network -- their employers, their families, and their own personal benefits. True to a pursuit of life, liberty, and happiness, the Guard instituted such programs as Employer Support of the Guard and Reserve (ESGR), an active duty role for the Guard members, and rebuilding the forces. Established in 1972, ESGR "promote[s] cooperation and understanding between Reserve Component Service members and their civilian employers and ... assist[s] in the resolution of conflicts arising from an employee's military commitment".[31] The establishment of ESGR reflected the Categorical Imperative in the local community as the Department of Defense reached out to ensure that

---

[30] Foreshadowing the events of 9/11, when the Guard would be called upon to perform both of its missions simultaneously – defending the nation at home in New York, Washington DC, and Shanksville, PA and then in Afghanistan.

[31] "About ESGR: Who is ESGR?" Employer Support of the Guard and Reserve, accessed March 7, 2019, https://www.esgr.mil/About-ESGR/Who-is-ESGR

employers and employees realized support in balancing the complex nature of the lives of their citizen-soldiers. In this manner, the employers were given the opportunity to fulfill their own "higher duty" in support of the National Guard and their local communities. Benefits that the active duty enjoyed were made available to the Guard and a more liberal medical and dental program was instituted. Most of these benefits were spearheaded and lobbied for by NGAUS – still a powerhouse on Capitol Hill as it had been in the Post-World War One and Two days, and dating all the way back to 1878. NGAUS would maintain its power consistently up to present day.

During the 1970s and '80s, the country began to depend on the Guard more and more for its domestic role and the Guard became famous for its missions in hurricane relief, flooding aid, wildfire suppression, and other natural disaster responses. Rebuilding its reputation from the ebb of the 1960s and early 1970s, the Guard became synonymous with rescue, aide, and family support. The disaster relief role played by the National Guard cannot be emphasized enough. It made the National Guard unique from any other American military service. As the Guard found itself in use overseas more and more, it also increased the domestic aid mission stateside. As the Enlightenment nature of the nation matured, the Guard fulfilled the "right to life, liberty, and the pursuit of happiness" by supporting the nation in international warfare as well as in its role at home focusing on the community. Embodying the Categorical Imperative in action, National Guardsmen continued the tradition of voluntarily joining the Guard to protect their homes and neighborhoods. A significant local support event in the recent history of the U.S. came in the early 1960s when an earthquake struck in Alaska. The bulk of the support provided by the Guard came in the form of airlift – and gave the Air National Guard an opportunity to shine. But that service became overshadowed by the turmoil of the Vietnam War and the civil rights disorder responses. However, the domestic mission continued to grow as governors became accustomed to calling in their state Guards for disaster relief missions.

By the 1980s, the Guard returned to support of the local community in full force. Along with a massive defense buildup directed by the Reagan administration, the Department of Defense implemented reviews of its structure. At the same time, adhering to the needs of the Army since the advent of Roundout the Guard emphasized training and efficiency on highly technical and up-to-date equipment, tanks, aircraft, and communications. This emphasis helped both the domestic missions and international readiness. Computers began to make inroads into the day-to-day lives of Guardsmen on the job as well as in uniform. In a fashion similar to the Scientific and Industrial revolutions of the nineteenth century, the late twentieth-century "information revolution" drastically changed communication and accountability. In

November, 1989, the Berlin Wall fell – symbolizing the end of the Cold War that had been the focus of American foreign policy since the end of World War Two. The United States was able to turn its attention away from containing the USSR within its borders and limiting its sphere of influence and to begin bringing its extended military forces home from Europe. To a lesser extent, the US was also able to bring troops home from the Asian front. The resulting pulling back of expenditure overseas as well as in the continental United States meant that the US realized a "peace dividend" in the 1990s. This peace dividend provided a much-needed opportunity for the National Guard and Congress to look inside and begin to build up support of family and community – a process that had begun in the early 70s. Riding on the wave of the Reagan-era buildup and the Clinton-era drawdown, the Department of Defense was able to take advantage of the peacetime world events. Congress implemented the enormously popular Active Guard and Reserve (AGR) Program that allowed part-time soldiers to serve volunteer active duty tours. These tours included following their active duty peers in overseas missions.[32] Specifically, in its role as the defender of National Guard interests, NGAUS was instrumental in lobbying for additional Guard benefits; increased recruitment reflected the proper treatment of the soldiers, their families, and their employers. Although this internal reflection and reorganization would carry on for at least the next decade, world events of 1990 put the un-tried Total Force Policy to the test.

Just as the United States realized it had "won" the Cold War, in August of 1990, Iraqi dictator Saddam Hussein invaded the neighboring country of Kuwait and the world returned to war. President George H. W. Bush, former ambassador to China and former head of the Central Intelligence Agency, was a consummate diplomat. Enlisting the approval of the United Nations, President Bush launched the entire "Total Force", including the Army and Air National Guard, in support of Operations Desert Shield and Storm ("ODS/S").[33] Led by General Colin Powell, the Joint Chiefs of Staff executed a long build up, a short and surgical war, and a long draw down. During ODS/S, the National Guard came into its own as an integral part of the Total Force. Not without its snags, the Guard assimilated into both the regular Army and the Air Force with little difficulty. The preparation provided by the Cold War proved useful. "Within 72 hours [of the Air Force calling for volunteers], more than twice the required

---

[32] Marion and Hoffman, *Forging a Total Force*, 64.

[33] For naming purposes, Operations Desert Shield and Storm worked like a donut. Operation Desert Shield refers to the deployment from August, 1990, to January, 1991. It also refers to the redeployment from the end of combat in February, 1991, to approximately August, 1991. Operation Desert Storm refers to the brief period of combat in the winter of 1991.

number came forward. About one week after the invasion, the first Air National Guard and Air Force Reserve C-141 Starlifters began ferrying American troops and equipment to Saudi Arabia".[34],[35] Astonishingly, "[d]uring [August] they carried out more than 40 percent of strategic airlift and one-third of aerial refueling missions.[36] The use of the National Guard became streamlined and "Air … Guard … leaders often accepted the activation of individuals and tailored small elements in place of their parent units.[37] In other words, particularly in the Air Guard, troops were surgically deployed as needed and inserted into otherwise active-duty units. In light of traditional confusion and standard disorganization in a massive international event like Operations Desert Shield and Storm, the deployment went surprisingly well and President G.H.W. Bush praised the effort, saying that the hangover of Vietnam was behind us.[38] This was good news, as it meant that the darkest period in the history of the National Guard had ended. Still stinging from the low point of public opinion during the Vietnam War, the National Guard had deployed, succeeded, and returned home to a jubilant, proud nation.

The Powell Doctrine, a name used to describe the deliberate and conscious effort at buildup and then the deliberate and conscious effort at breakdown, required another six months for the National Guard and active duty forces to return home. Although the public reception of the returning soldiers was positive and upbeat, employers and families made it clear to the Department of Defense that they had missed their deployed servicemembers. Upon return, the upper echelon of the American military – hearing the cries from the National Guard in particular – "designated the National Guard as the lead agent for family support and required National Guard and Army Reserve

---

[34] Marion and Hoffman, *Forging a Total Force*, 71.

[35] The Air Force Reserves are an entirely different reserve force that, with the National Guard, make up the "reserve component." Reservists are part time soldiers and airmen serving as Federal backup to the standing Army, Air Force, Navy, and Marines.

[36] Ibid.

[37] Ibid., 72.

[38] George H. W. Bush, President of the United States, "Remarks to the American Legislative Exchange Council" (video), 1 March 1991, accessed March 18, 2019, http://vandv reader.org/george-h-w-bush-proclaims-a-cure-for-the-vietnam-syndrome-01-march-1991/. The President makes the pertinent statement at the 8:58 point in the video. Coined by Secretary of State Henry Kissinger and President Ronald Reagan, "Vietnam Syndrome" began its life as a precursor to Post Traumatic Stress Syndrome ("PTSD") but would become the term used for hesitance to send American troops into combat in international theatres in fear of negative public opinion. "Vietnam Syndrome", *The Vietnam War*, accessed March 19, 2019, https://thevietnamwar.info/vietnam-syndrome/ After President G.H.W. Bush referred to it, later interpretations called the syndrome the "Vietnam Hangover" which has since earned common popular usage.

commanders to operate family assistance programs".[39] Equally important, the Guard saw to the needs of local employers who, by law, had to keep the jobs of deployed Guardsmen available for them upon their return. The greatest need for employers involved back filling positions while the Guardsmen were gone and continuing to pay Guardsmen while they were overseas. "Most employers supported their reservists and many went beyond their legal obligations".[40] In a very real way, this support from the established community was an additional example of the Categorical Imperative at work – beyond the purview of the Guard soldier, the employers and families engaged in their own performance in service to a higher duty. Their actions in support of the National Guard were universal, fair, and unmanipulative. Kant, estranged from his own family, may not have envisioned such a literal "universality" although he must have understood the application would be timeless and complete.

After the war, the United States found itself in welcome period of peace. The time was ripe for the federal government to start reevaluating needs based on the Peace Dividend and the breakup of the Soviet Union. Between 1996 and 1997, the military underwent a Quadrennial Review – including a "Bottom Up Review" and a Base Realignment and Closure ("BRAC"). A few very important things happened in this period of time that must be mentioned in order to understand the importance of the Categorical Imperative and the Kantian moral law as it flowed through National Guard service. The National Guard maintained its dual role as a domestic disaster response force as well as maintaining deployable readiness. The Guard also began to see itself moving away from being a strategic reserve -- its duty starting to involve more than merely supporting local communities. During this period, the Guard initiated a program called the State Partnership Program – spurred by the end of the Cold War, Michigan, Pennsylvania, and Maryland partnered with the three Baltic states, Latvia, Lithuania, and Estonia. The states and the countries developed partnerships, shared military training knowledge and, important for the current argument, shared Citizen-soldier roles. A typical Guardsman who deployed to his sister country might show the soldiers of that country how to fire a weapon, or even set up a beehive for agricultural development. The Guard began to see itself as an operational force – shoulder to shoulder with their active duty peers. The Gulf War success had taught that the Guard was capable of performing duties overseas that they also performed at home. Also, growing unrest in the Balkans began to reveal that the standing army had grown to rely on the National Guard. The reliance was so strong that "[t]he new paradigm went a step further in the long-running Joint Guardian operation, in which

---

[39] Marion and Hoffman, *Forging a Total Force*, 80.
[40] Ibid., 81.

[Army National Guard] divisions from Pennsylvania, Indiana, California, Texas, and Virginia contributed units for six-month tours of duty, spelling regular brigades in the rotation".[41] By spelling the regular brigades, the National Guard was able to relieve the active duty from constant duty. Over time and by the end of the Balkan unrest, the Citizen-soldier forces were uniformly Air National Guard and demonstrated the new integration between the National Guard and the active duty.

For the Categorical Imperative to have at its core a universally fair and unmanipulative act, it has to be timeless. The Categorical Imperative followed the men and women of the National Guard from 1636 and, while the Guard certainly changed, the moral duty remained the same. In the case of the modern military of the twentieth and twenty-first centuries, the key point is their voluntary nature. It is important to understand that, even in the difficult draft periods of the Vietnam conflict, membership in the National Guard was always voluntary. Once a soldier on a traditional state status, one could certainly be involuntarily put into federal status – but the universal nature of the decision to join the Guard in the first place never changed. Those Americans who chafed at the involuntary nature of federalization needed only be reminded of their decision to join the Guard in peacetime in order to end the conversation. This serious and sobering fact was never so important as on September 11, 2001. From a moral duty and a National Guard standpoint, the Guard had not been called upon to defend home soil and local communities since the seventeenth and eighteenth centuries the way the Guard was that day. Then, within a month, the National Guard was called upon to throw off any remaining hint of being a strategic reserve force – and enter the international world of warfare once again. September 11, 2001, marked a unique day for the National Guard – one in which the Guard not only performed its duty as the first responders in time of domestic emergency but also on the front lines of a foreign war Americans could not have known would last for 18 years and counting.

The morning of September 11th is well-documented and likely known to the readers of this book. The National Guard response to the aircraft as they crashed into the World Trade Center, NY; the Pentagon, VA; and a field in Shanksville, PA, was immediate. Even today, audio recording of the Boston Center air traffic control as they realize they will have to alert the military is chilling. While the exact timeline involving the Guard is unknown, the military was alerted through US domestic and North American Aerospace Defense (NORAD) protocols. The National Guard did respond within minutes to the call. Over 3,000 fatalities from a terrorist attack on American soil mobilized almost

---

[41] Ibid., 83.

every aspect of the National Guard and the first responder forces. In particular, the New York National Guard, 69th Regiment Armory at Lexington Avenue responded to the domestic emergency. New York immediately mobilized over 6,000 Guardsmen and Washington, DC, mobilized over 600.[42] On the morning of 9/11, as American Airlines Flight 77 impacted the west side of the Pentagon, DC Air National Guard F-16s on a routine training mission were activated, refueled, and armed. Airborne again, they were ordered to confront any commercial aircraft not in compliance with the air traffic control orders to land. The Pennsylvania Army National Guard, 104th Aviation Regiment flew Governor Tom Ridge to the crash site in Shanksville, PA that morning. National Guard Air Wings supplied manpower and aircraft to fly Combat Air Patrols over major cities in the United States. Within the next few days, Virginia, Indiana, New Jersey, Louisiana, and numerous other states joined in the effort. Foreshadowing the creation of the Department of Homeland Security (DHS), the Coast Guard (often confused with the National Guard) "became responsible for tightening security at some 350 U.S. ports".[43] Originally under the Department of Transportation, the Coast Guard would be moved to DHS upon that agency's creation – where the Coast Guard remains to this day.[44] Within months of the attack, thousands more Guardsmen were put on duty in domestic airports, train stations, and other main hubs of transportation. The universal, fair, and straightforward nature of Kant's Categorical Imperative is best viewed at this moment in American history. While the Utilitarian argument for the morality of the citizen-soldier model in a democratic republic had appealed to the command structure of the National Guard and the Congress since the eighteenth century, 9/11 left no room for arguing about cost effectiveness and the ability of the National Guard to meet statistical readiness numbers. Instead, its exigencies brought forward the essential duty-based nature of voluntary service in the military. Coming almost full circle, on 9/11/2001, the Guard's voluntary nature returned to the fact that the Guard was responding to attacks on U.S. soil—defending the homeland as it had originally been envisioned to do. On that day and moving forward, American soldiers and airmen rose to the occasion to protect and defend the right of all citizens to pursue life (most importantly), liberty, and the pursuit of happiness.

---

[42] Ibid., 99.

[43] Ibid., 100.

[44] Although routinely confused with each other, the Coast Guard serves under the Department of Homeland Security (and formerly under the Department of Transportation) because Coast Guard officials have police powers. The National Guard does not – as specifically prohibited by *Posse Comitatus*.

After 9/11 and the development of the DHS, the role of the National Guard in local police enforcement acts needed to be clarified. In a manner similar to the reports written after the civil disorder of the 1960s and early 1970s, the Guard, the Federal government, and the state governments tried to define the Guard's role in domestic terrorism force protection. Ever wary of the 1878 *Posse Comitatus* statute, which remained unchanged from the nineteenth century, the Guard's role was strictly limited to support of local constabularies. The Guard itself pushed back against its over-use in domestic police assistance operations and, in 2002 after 5,000 Guardsmen helped make the Utah Olympics secure, Major General John Kane, ID, as the Chairman of NGAUS' sister organization, the Adjutant General Association of the United States (AGAUS)[45] stated his opinion that routine federalization of the National Guard in this manner would erode state control by the governors.[46] Within months of 9/11, the National Guard – now fulfilling General Dick's vision of total incorporation into the standing army while maintaining the unique nature of its own structure – deployed en masse to war in Afghanistan. The Total Force Policy was finally going to be tested with extreme measures. Little did the National Guard know, the test was only beginning. By 2003, a second front opened in Iraq. The National Guard, no longer a strategic reserve, would serve in Operation Enduring Freedom (OEF) in Afghanistan, and Operation Iraqi Freedom (OIF) for the next nearly two decades. The focus on the homeland continued to be a part of the National Guard mission – and served to demonstrate the strength of the Kantian Categorical Imperative in action as the troops spread thinly across the globe fighting two wars while also fighting fires, earthquakes, and hurricanes within the Continental United States. By this time, barriers to service like gender, race, or religion had been removed, allowing more citizens to serve. Heeding the advantages of service in the National Guard but also that Kantian moral duty, Guardsmen transitioned routinely between performing their missions in OEF and OIF and their domestic missions at home. Major (ret). MJ Hegar a helicopter pilot in the California Air National Guard served as an example of someone able and willing to perform a combat mission overseas as well as a counter-drug and search and rescue missions in the United States. In 2005, when Hurricane Katrina roared into the Gulf Coast of Louisiana

---

[45] Founded in 1912, also in response to the Wickersham Decision that the Guard could not be deployed outside the United States borders, AGAUS was and is comprised of the Adjutant Generals (commanding generals) of the National Guard in each state, territory, and the District of Columbia. Like NGAUS, AGAUS is a lobbying organization but with the power of boots on the ground in the respective states they represent. It is pronounced, Ay-Jee-AY-You-Ess.

[46] Kristin Patterson, "President Urged to Keep Guardsmen Under State Control," *National Guard*, March/April 2002, 14.

destroying life, liberty, and property for the entire population, National Guardsmen from all over the country rose to the occasion – despite supporting the two ongoing wars overseas. The National Guard response to Katrina was the largest coordinated disaster relief effort in the entire history of the National Guard. The entire fifty-four states, territories, and the District of Columbia raced to the aid of New Orleans, LA. In all, over 50,000 Guardsmen responded to the emergency. The Army Guard rescued 17,000 people and the Air National Guard evacuated 70,000.

Over the ensuing years of wars in Afghanistan and Iraq, as well as the mission at home, NGAUS continued to lobby on behalf of the interests of the National Guard soldiers and airmen. One of the most significant, landmark events in the recent history of the Guard occurred in two parts – the first in 2008 as preparation for the second in 2011. The highest-ranking officers in the United States military during peacetime are general officers who wear four stars on their shoulders.[47] Given the nature and responsibilities placed on the National Guard since 9/11, Congress granted the first four-star billet to Air National Guard General Craig R. McKinley. He became the Chief of the National Guard Bureau (NGB) and, within three years, was appointed to the Joint Chiefs of Staff (JCS). The National Guard, as of 2011, was now fully represented on the JCS and of equal rank with Army, Air Force, Navy, and Marine peers. NGAUS and many in the Guard viewed this appointment as the jewel in the crown of the Total Force Policy and the culmination of General Dick's dream in 1903 (had he been able to imagine such a role for the National Guard). Lieutenant Colonel Judd Mahfouz of the Louisiana National Guard describes the General's current role thus:

> We are not a service, but rather a Joint Activity of the Department of Defense (per the Charter). The Chief's role as a JCS member is not only military advice, but also to articulate the role of the non-federal NG, and to serve as a channel of communications between DoD and the National Guards of the 50 states, 3 territories, and the District of Columbia. These roles as statutory and established in the JSPS [Joint Strategic Planning System] and The NGB Charter. Under the Empowerment Act (which made the CNGB a Four-Star), he also has a statutory obligation to train the militia to federal standards.[48]

---

[47] Historically, there have been few five star generals – including Army generals John J. Pershing, Dwight D. Eisenhower, and Omar Bradley, and Air Force general Hap Arnold.
[48] Lt Col Judd D. Mahfouz, Chief, Strategy Development Branch, NG JS J59-SD, LA ARNG, email message to author, February 26, 2019.

The President of NGAUS, Major General Gus Hargett, (ret. Adjutant General, TN), presided over the negotiations during the promotion and appointment of General Craig R. McKinley. In an interview, Major General Hargett stated that his belief in the Guard as an operational fighting force overseas and an operational first responder force within the United States was reflected in his service of over 47 years in the Tennessee Army National Guard, culminating as the commanding general of the state force.

> First and foremost, the Guard is the primary combat reserve of the Army and the Air Force. The Guard also has the capability to do standalone combat operations and in many cases are the only component with certain essential capabilities. A perfect example is the Air Defense Batteries that provide Air Defense for the National Capitol Region.[49]

With this observation, General Hargett demonstrated the use of today's National Guard – both in its international capacity as the primary combat reserve but also as a unique force with domestic defense capability. All bear tribute to our Enlightenment roots – with man-power and expertise provided by the citizen-soldier who volunteers his time to defend his community's right to pursue life, liberty, and happiness. The Kantian Categorical Imperative has extended to family and employer support as well. General Hargett noted,

> I have witnessed this first hand…When we mobilized the Engineer unit from Union City, Tennessee Goodyear Tire and Rubber, one of the larger employers in the community hug a flag over each employee's work position and voluntarily mowed their yards and help[ed] the spouse with whatever their needs were.[50]

Following General McKinley's tenure as Chief of the National Guard Bureau and a member of the Joint Chiefs of Staff, General Frank Grass, Army National Guard, assumed the role. It was General Grass who was able to settle into the position and carve out the nature of the position with the advantage of experience. Both Generals Hargett and Grass noted in their interviews that in their lifetimes, the Guard had viewed itself as a second-class citizen – but by

---

[49] Gus Hargett, Major General (Ret.), Adjutant General of Tennessee, President, National Guard Association of the United States, answers to questionnaire by author, Nashville, December 15, 2018.
[50] Ibid.

2011, this citizen-soldier branch had attained the respect of its peer services.[51] During his time as the Chief of NGB, General Grass served under Defense Secretaries Panetta, Hagel, and Carter. Issues facing General Grass included the attempted drawdown of OEF and OIF – which were interrupted by the Russian annexation of Crimea, and the rise of ISIS in Iraq. As General Grass put it, "The enemy always gets a vote".[52] Additionally, US military attention was 'pivoting' toward Asia. Domestically, the Department of Defense had to deal with a belt-tightening Act of Congress known as Sequestration in 2013 as well as an Executive Branch effort to "reprioritize federal spending [away from the military and toward] education, infrastructure, healthcare, etc."[53] As for his role on the JCS, General Grass explained his critical impact,

> My first thought was I needed to add value to the Secretary of Defense, the Chairman and the Joint Chiefs. [T]He CNGB role on the JCS was tested only about two months in the job when Super Storm Sandy hit the East Coast. I spent about eight hours over two weeks in meetings with Secretary Leon Panera [sic] … as we prepared … the Secretary for his meetings at the White House….I received frequent updates from the Adjutants General affected by Super Storm Sandy and relayed that information directly to Secretary Panetta and/or his Assistant Secretary of Homeland Security. Additionally, the staff and I had frequent communications with the NORTHCOM Commander and staff, and FEMA. This homeland event and many others; such as the Boston Marathon bombing, Ferguson and Baltimore unrest, South Carolina and Missouri historic flooding, and western wildfires proved the value of CNGB as a member of the CJCS.[54]

This relationship became absolutely indispensable for the National Guard and for the nation as a whole as the country began to rely more and more on its Citizen-soldiers. The citizen-soldier, in return (including General Grass himself) forged ahead supporting the nation in order to support the local communities. The dual mission of the National Guard – domestic and international – finally reached the highest corridors of power while providing a constant reminder of the fundamental unit of power in the nation, the local

---

[51] In my personal experience, the Guard still calls itself the "raggedy-ass militia."
[52] Frank P. Grass, General (Ret.), Chief, National Guard Bureau, Member, Joint Chiefs of Staff, answers to questionnaire by author, St. Louis, November 16, 2018.
[53] Ibid.
[54] Ibid.

community supported by its own citizens willing to take up arms to protect their own and their fellow citizens' pursuit of life, liberty, and happiness.

Thus, as the present-day arrives at the doorstep, the Categorical Imperative remains unperturbed – from 1636 to 2019, the Citizen-soldier serves his community voluntarily and at the behest of a duly elected legislature. The Enlightenment theory of Immanuel Kant that applies universally, regardless of circumstances or outcome, holds true to the higher duty of protecting one's community from enemies without and within. In particular, this chapter has shown that the modern world, saturated with the high cost of mutually assured destruction and the benefits of peace and prosperity brought on by a smaller and smaller global community, still relies on the empowered individual to protect his rights and the rights of others. At the end of the day, human dignity and free will form the basis of serving your country both as a citizen and a soldier. In this application, the moral law, as described by Immanuel Kant, is truly universal, fairly served, and a means unto itself. The following Conclusion will draw together the various applications of this duty to the Citizen-soldier model across the different periods of U.S. history in a brief summary. The Conclusion will review and strengthen the central theme of this book: that a Deontological argument, though less used than Utilitarian justifications, can provide as powerful a philosophical underpinning for the National Guard and its continued role in America's military policy.

Conclusion

Over almost four hundred years of history, the National Guard of the United States remains an example of an Enlightenment theory put to the test. That Enlightenment theory, Kant's Categorical Imperative, can be favorable applied to every aspect of the history of the National Guard. Broadly speaking, Kant's Categorical Imperative, a moral law that must comply with universal application, fairness, and no use of a man as a means to an end, is an ideal that started with the trayned-bands of the 17ᵗʰ Century and remained true throughout the evolution of the United States and her role in the global community.

With an emphasis by Kant on human dignity and autonomy of free will, service in the local militias depended on a voting population able to elect legislators who, in turn, legislated part-time membership in the militia for mutual protection. Beginning in 1636, before Kant was even born, the colonists of the North American continent elected officials who recognized a need for protection for their fledgling villages from attacking local indigenous people as well as various fauna. On December 13, 1636, in Salem, MA, the first formally legislated Muster occurred on the village green – setting the stage for what would become one of the most formidable fighting forces of the 21ˢᵗ Century. Kant's Categorical Imperative was articulated in his *Critique of Practical Reason*, published in 1788. Before reaching this stage, Kant wrote the *Groundwork of the Metaphysics of Morals* published in 1785. According to the editor of *The Cambridge Edition of the Works of Immanuel Kant: Practical Philosophy*, Allen W. Wood, "*The Groundwork* … is not only a step in fulfilling Kant's project of a metaphysics of morals, but also an eloquent defense of enlightenment and self-directing reason…."[1] He expounds,

> The moral law is the only conceivable source of obligation because it is a principle of *autonomy*, which recognizes no law except what rational beings give themselves a priori through their own reason – a reason that is entirely self-directing, free of any guidance by natural impulse, social tradition, religious revelation, or poetic inspiration. It is this capacity to be unconditionally legislative that constitutes the dignity (absolute and incomparable worth) of humanity.[2]

---

[1] Wood, *The Cambridge Edition of the Works of Immanuel Kant: Practical Philosophy*, xxii.
[2] Ibid.

In *Groundwork*, Kant formulated various definitions of the Categorical Imperative including the Formula of Universal Law, the Formula of the law of Nature, and the Formula of Humanity.[3] Although separate calculations, they combined into a three-prong basis for evaluation. Simply put, for a moral law to be a Categorical Imperative that action must be universally applicable, viewed as fair by all the parties involved, and not use men as a means to an end. Such a formulation provides the reader with the ability to then determine whether a specific act is a moral law. In the case of the present book, Kant's reliance on human dignity and the autonomy of free will was performed by electing legislatures to govern with the approval of the electorate. In 1789 the Founding Fathers were able to incorporate such a quintessential theory into the very fabric of the Constitution of the United States. During the first rough decades in the fledgling nation, service in the Militias was seen as necessary for the protection of the local community and was legislated by the elected leaders routinely. The early volunteer Militias depended wholly on u service being universally expected, perceived as fair, and an end unto itself.

During the Revolutionary War, General George Washington realized that the Colonies could not prevail against the substantially better kitted British Army without enlisting the aid of full-time soldiers with extensive training. Having served in the Virginia Militia himself, General Washington was well aware of the hardships and sacrifices made by the citizens who were willing to take up arms to protect their interests and those of their fellow men. While the Militias formed necessary aid and augmentation, the new Continental Army of 1775 led the way. Service in the militias, significantly, was viewed all the more as critical to the support of local communities. The Continental Army fought across state lines and over great distance while the Militias protected their local communities. By the early 19th Century, after the victory of the Colonies over the British and various ensuing skirmishes, the Militias remained active and began to seek recognition in the halls of the young Federal government. Meanwhile, the early 18th Century led to a period of growth and expansion for the young nation that increased the communication of Enlightenment theory through a network of colleges and Universities. The blossoming schools of philosophy in Europe spread to the new country and took on their own character. Americans, faced with a rugged new territory to the West, began to move beyond the colonies and to encounter an environment similar to the one found by their predecessors in the previous century. Voluntary service in protection of the community remained a significant part of the social fabric.

---

[3] See also: *The Categorical Imperative: A Study in Kant's Moral Philosophy*, H. J. Paton (New York: Harper, 1947), Book III, pp. 129-128.

The country was torn apart in the mid-19th Century by a brutal Civil War that brought the many militias into war with each other, famously described as brother-against-brother. Without structure to the militias, is it nearly impossible to apply the Categorical Imperative to the foundation of the National Guard – during the Civil War the roots of the National Guard as we come to know it was pulled up by the secessionist states. Amidst the chaos and confusion, the concept of the Militias was smothered. By the end of the Civil War, however, the National Guard began to reform – to build itself back into a recognizable Militia force. At this point, the Guard realized it stood a good chance of being assimilated into the Standing Army and that the many states would no longer have their own military forces to defend their interests. Unwilling to let that happen, the General officer corps united to form the National Guard Association of the United States in 1878. NGAUS' mission was to ensure the survivability of the National Guard as a viable fighting force at the state level. In order to accomplish their mission, they moved the headquarters to Washington DC and began to lobby in the halls of Congress. General Charles Dick, himself a National Guardsman from Ohio, sponsored The Dick Act of 1903 which would serve as a launching pad for the establishment of the National Guard as the primary reserve force for the standing Army. The Dick Act and the efforts leading up to its passage demonstrate the universality of the citizen-soldier concept in a democratic republic. Founded on Enlightenment theory, duly elected officials created a statutory method to protect the existence of a volunteer military service that was based on grassroots efforts to protect the local community.

By 1916 however, the world began to become complicated and the mission of the National Guard had to evolve with it. Having been freed during the Civil War, the negro community effectively began a diaspora across the United States. A lack of proper response by the Federal and state governments led to uneasy integration – which in turn led to violent civil disorder. The states resorted to using the National Guard to quell the social disruptions. Along with a domestic mission, the Guard was appealing for the Federal government to want to use to augment their interests overseas. In an unusual crossover, when the United States entered World War One in 1917, the African Americans in New York and the upper East Coast saw an opportunity to volunteer for service overseas. In fact, they represented an example of Kant's Categorical Imperative in action – they entered into service voluntarily with little or no hope of concrete social advancement or recognition. They may have hoped for better treatment in the US when they returned, but their service represented a pure voluntary willingness to serve to protect their local community interests fairly and as a means to its own end. World War Two brought the Guard back overseas by the hundreds of thousands. By the 1950s, women began to serve in the same capacity as the African Americans had – not necessarily welcome and certainly not equal to their white male peers but serving with a sense of a higher duty. The 1950s also brought the beginning of the Civil Rights movement in the United States. In 1948, President Harry S. Truman, himself a National Guardsman, integrated the military services. The military struggled along with the rest of the nation as the Civil Rights act of 1964 became the law of the land.

As with any ideal like the Categorical Imperative, actual measurements of attaining it reflect ebbs and flows. The National Guard ebbed in the 1960s when the Johnson Administration elected not to send them overseas with the regular army to serve in Vietnam. Incursions into Cambodia and Laos, against international agreements, contributed to making the War unpopular with the citizenry of the United States. Violent civil disorder broke out countrywide and the National Guard was often called in to quash it. Not only were the soldiers not serving overseas, they were viewed as the enemy on home soil. Combined with the civil disorder of the Vietnam protestors, the view that the National Guard was nothing more than a way to defer service in the war, and the National Guard participation quashing civil rights riots, the Guard's reputation sunk to an historic low. It is important to realize that the Categorical Imperative did not change --- those who served still heard the calling of the moral duty to protect their communities. The leadership of the US Military recognized a need for change and began to implement a new theory of service – the Total Force Policy. Maintaining its dual mission both at home and increasingly overseas, the Guard began to serve with its active-duty counterpart in Western Europe during the breakup of the former Soviet Union. As one of the best examples of the Categorical Imperative at work, the State Partnership Program (SPP) paired National Guard units from individual states, territories, and the District of Columbia with former Soviet satellites as they just began to emerge from behind the Iron Curtain. Maryland, Pennsylvania, and Michigan paired with the tiny Baltic countries, Latvia, Lithuania, and Estonia to exchange military aid and training. With both sides learning from each other, peace and tranquility were more than likely to give advantage to the now global community.

In 1990 the beginning of Operation Desert Shield and Storm put the Total Force Policy to the test and the outbreak of war in the Balkans in 1991 gave the Guard another opportunity to serve with its active-duty counterpart but by less peaceful means. Like the Militia soldiers of the 17th century, volunteer Guardsmen served their communities and the best interests of the society at large. Such service was deemed fair and men were not used as a means to an end. The attacks on New York City, Shanksville, and Washington, DC, on September 11, 2001, changed the world – but did not change the role of the National Guard or the Kantian moral law to serve. In fact, the Guard was at the forefront of both its dual missions on that day and the months to follow. The dire emergencies of that morning brought the Guard out in full force defending communities and neighborhoods as they suffered through the violent moments of the crashing aircraft and the fallout. In a practical return to the 17th Century, Guardsmen found themselves "meeting on the village green to protect their community under immediate threat". Within days, they were kitted out and sent to Afghanistan in Operation Enduring Freedom – an Operation augmented by Operation Iraqi freedom three years later. Although OIF has terminated, OEF continues to this day. It is significant to note that the National Guard Association of the United States, founded in 1878, continues to play its role as the civilian watchdog ensuring that the interests of the citizen-soldiers are protected on Capitol Hill through lobbying for healthcare benefits, proper treatment of the civilian employers, and the families. By so doing the National Guard comes together both as citizens and as soldiers to protect their service – thereby ensuring that voluntary service and its need is viewed as fair and as a means to its own end. Such attention of care dedicated to employers, families, and the service members themselves has improved over the past years thanks to NGAUS.

Looking back, over approximately 400 years of history, it is safe to say that the citizen-soldier concept of military service comports with the Enlightenment-born theory of government-granted authority by the governed in a democratic republic. That service – duty as both a citizen and a protector of the community interests fit into Kant's Enlightenment theory of the moral law or Categorical Imperative, in all of its parts. First, that duty to serve is timeless and unchanging. Demonstrated in the last one hundred pages of narrative, one can readily see that the ideal of the Categorical Imperative doesn't change – the citizen-soldier voluntarily serves his or her community either at his own behest or the behest of those legislators whose authority he or took part in granting. As seen in the 1960s, even when the ideal was not attained, the moral law still applied. Although the numbers of volunteers in the National Guard rose and fell over time, the Federal and state governments always saw them as a significant part of the total number of soldiers needed to defend the nation. Clearly, service was deemed by those in uniform as fair – the idea of mutual security needs to be applied to the Guard as evenly as to any military service. Even at its lowest ebb, in the 1960s, the Guard still filled the ranks when needed. Finally, the National Guardsman's service, over time, has been demonstrated as a means unto itself. Striving never to use the Guardsman as a means to an end, the United States National Guard from its inception as a village militia in1636 and onward to the formidable fighting force it is today as the National Guard of the United States has never lost focus on each person's service. Whether stuffing sandbags, dropping fire retardant on Western wildfires, supporting earthquake victims, or quelling civil disorder all the way to taking part in the Total Force Policy and fighting shoulder to shoulder in foreign wars with the regular army, truly the Categorical Imperative in action – the National Guard is always ready, always there.

Bibliography

Abbot, W. W., ed. *The Papers of George Washington: Colonial Series volume 1, 1748- August, 1755.* Charlottesville and London: University Press of Virginia, 1983.

Adams, Charles Francis, ed., *Works of John Adams, vol. 5 (Defence of the Constitutions Vols. 11 and III, 1851).* Accessed April 3, 2019. https://oll.libertyfund.org/titles/adams-the-works-of-john-adams-vol-5-defence-of-the-constitutions-vols-ii-and-iii

Anonymous photo. (Accessed July 27, 2018). http://theoldstonehouse.org/history/battle-of-brooklyn/.

Aquinas, St. Thomas. *Summa Theologiae.* Translated by Fathers of the English Dominican Province, 1920. Online Edition: 2017. Accessed April 10, 2019. http://www.newadvent.org/summa/3040.htm#article1.

Audi, Robert, ed. *The Cambridge Dictionary of Philosophy, 3rd Edition.* New York: Cambridge University Press, 2015.

Augustine of Hippo. *City of God,* translated by Henry Bettenson. London: Penguin Classics, 2004.

Arendt, Hannah. *The Portable Hannah Arendt.* Edited by Peter Baehr. New York: Penguin Classics, 2000.

Breslaw, Elaine G. "Enlightened Marylanders: Scientific Interests of pre-Revolutionary Times". *Maryland Historical Magazine,* Spring/Sumer, 2018.

Bush, George H. W., President of the United States. "Remarks to the American Legislative Exchange Council 1 March 1991" (video). Uploaded by James Mckay, January 11, 2018. Accessed February 11, 2019. http://vandvreader.org/george-h-w-bush-proclaims-a-cure-for-the-vietnam-syndrome-01-march-1991/

Clark, E. Culpepper. *The Schoolhouse Door: Segregation's Last Stand at the University of Alabama.* Oxford: Oxford University Press, 1993.

Clements, S. Eugene, and F. Edward Wright. *The Maryland Militia in the Revolutionary War.* Westminster, MD: Heritage Books, 2006.

Cone, Spencer W., ed. *The United States Democratic Review,* Jan-Jun, 1839. Accessed July 19, 2018. https://babel.hathitrust.org/cgi/pt?id=mdp.39015035929606;view=1up;seq=426.

Correll, John T. "Origins of the Total Force." *Air Force Magazine,* February, 2011.

Creighton Abrams, speech given September 11, 1973 for TRADOC/FORSCOM Chaplain Training Conference, Kansas City, MO.

De Villers, Charles Francois Dominique. *Philosophie de Kant.* Metz: chez Collignon, 1801.

Doubler, Michael D. *Civilian in Peace, Soldier in War.* Lawrence: University of Kansas Press, 2003.

Dunbar, Donald P., Major General. 2018. "Legislative History of the National Guard." Lecture presented at the National Guard Association of the United States Meeting of the Board of Directors, November 16.

Employer Support of the Guard and Reserve. "About ESGR: Who is ESGR?" Employer Support of the Guard and Reserve. (Accessed March 7, 2019). https://www.esgr.mil/About-ESGR/Who-is-ESGR.

Forbes Letters. National Guard Memorial Museum, Library, and Archives, Washington, D.C.

Gadamer, Hans-Georg. *Truth and Method, 2nd Revised Edition.* Translated by Joel Weinsheimer and Donald G. Marshall. New York: Continuum, 2004.

George C. Marshall Foundation. "Marshall and the Civilian Conservation Corps.", (Accessed February 15, 2019). https://www.marshallfoundation.org/blog/marshall-civilian-conservation-corps/

Grass, Frank, General, (Ret.), 2d Four Star General in the National Guard of the United States, Chief, National Guard Bureau, and Member of the Joint Chiefs of Staff, written questionnaire by author, St. Louis, November 16, 2018.

Gross, Charles J. and Susan Rosenfeld. *Air National Guard at 60: A History.* Washington, D.C.: Department of the Air Force, 2007.

Hamilton, Edith. *Mythology.* Boston: Little, Brown & Company, 1942.

Hargett, Gus, Major General (Ret.), former Adjutant General of Tennessee and President of the National Guard Association of the United States, written questionnaire by author, Nashville, December 15, 2018.

Independent Inquirer and Commercial Advertiser (Providence), August 26, 1824.

Kant, Immanuel. *Critique of Practical Reason.* Cambridge: Cambridge University Press, 2013.

Kant, Immanuel. *The Cambridge Edition of the Works of Immanuel Kant: Practical Philosophy.* General Editors, Paul Guyer and Allan W. Wood. Edited and translated by Mary J. Gregor. New York: Cambridge University Press, 2008.

Kuhn, Thomas. *The Structure of Scientific Revolutions.* Chicago: University of Chicago Press, 1962.

Locke, John. *The Second Treatise of Government.* Mineola: Dover Publications, 2002.

Lossing, Benson J. and George C. Strong. *Cadet life at West Point/By an officer of the United States army. With a descriptive sketch of West Point.* Boston: T.O.H.P. Burnham, 1862. Accessed March 4, 2019. http://digital-library.usma.edu/cdm/ref/collection/p16919coll10/id/4270

Maddow, Rachel. *Drift.* New York: Crown Publishers, 2012.

Mahfouz, Judd D. Chief, Strategy Development Branch, NG JS J59-SD, LA ARNG, email message to author, February 26, 2019.

Malone, Dumas. *Jefferson and the Rights of Man.* Boston: Little, Brown and Company, 1951.

Marion, Forrest L. and Jon T. Hoffman. *Forging a Total Force.* Washington, D.C.: Historical Office, Office of the Secretary of Defense, 2018.

Matloff, Maurice, ed. *American Military History.* Washington D.C.: U.S. Army Office of the Chief of Military History, 1969.

National Association of Attorneys General, Committee on the Office of Attorney General. *Legal Issues Concerning the Role of the National Guard in Civil Disorders: Staff Report to the Special Committee on Legal Services to Military Forces.* Washington D.C.: General Printing Office, 1973.

Old Stone House Walking Tour. (Accessed July 27, 2018). http://theoldstone house.org/wp-content/uploads/2016/01/Battle-Brooklyn-walking-tour.pdf

Paton, H. J. *The Categorical Imperative.* Philadelphia: University of Pennsylvania Press, 1947.

Patterson, Kristin. "President Urged to Keep Guardsmen Under State Control." *National Guard,* March/April, 2002.

Pogue, Forrest C. *George C. Marshall: Education of a General.* New York: Viking Press, 1963.

Proceedings of the Conventions of the Province of Maryland held at the City of Annapolis, 1774, 1775, & 1776. Baltimore: James Lucas & E. K. Deaver, Annapolis—Jonas Green, 1836. Accessed July 26, 2018. https://ia800202.us. archive.org/1/items/proceedingsofcon00mary/proceedingsofcon00mary.pdf.

Riley, Ken. *Lafayette and the National Guard,* April 1989, acrylic, 18 x 24 inches, Arlington,

National Guard Bureau, United States Pentagon.

Rohn, Alan. "Vietnam Syndrome." *The Vietnam War,* June 27, 2014. (Accessed July 10, 2019). https://thevietnamwar.info/vietnam-syndrome/

Schleiermacher, Friedrich. "Second Speech on the Nature of Religion", *On Religion,* trans. John Oman (New York, 1958).

Shurtleff, Nathaniel B., MD, ed. *Records of the Governor and Company of the Massachusetts Bay in New England,* Vol. 1, 1628-1641. Boston: The Press of William White, 1853.

Smith, Mike R. "Guardmembers remember Oklahoma City bombing." Army.mil, April 19, 2010. (Accessed July 6, 2018). https://www.army.mil/ article/37587/guardmembers_remember_oklahoma_city_bombing

Sorley, Lewis. "The Way of the Soldier: Remembering General Creighton Abrams." *Foreign Policy Research Institute,* May 30, 2013. (Accessed April 2, 2019). https://www.fpri.org/article/2013/05/the-way-of-the-soldier-remem bering-general-creighton-abrams/

Sorley, Lewis. *Thunderbolt: General Creighton Abrams and the Army of His Times.* Bloomington: Indiana University Press, 2008.

Stanford Encyclopedia of Philosophy. "Immanuel Kant." (Accessed May 2, 2019). https://plato.standford.edu/archives/sum2018/entries/kant/

Stivison, David V., ed. *Magna Carta in America.* Baltimore: Gateway Press, Inc. 1993.

Swinton, William. *History of the Seventh Regiment, National Guard.* New York: Bields, Osgood, & Co., 1870.

Tharp, Charles, great-grandson of Senator Charles W. F. Dick (R-OH), written questionnaire by author, Baltimore, August 20, 2018.

Trainor, Ryan P. Archivist/Museum Specialist, National Guard Educational Foundation, e-mail message to author, July 27, 2018.

Tyler, Lyon G., ed. "Early Courses and Professors at William and Mary College." *The William and Mary Quarterly,* Vol. XIV, no. 2 (October, 1905): 75. Accessed August 8, 2018. https://play.google.com/books/reader?id=gCYjAQAAIAAJ& printsec=frontcover&output=reader&hl=en&pg=GBS.PR1

Underdal, Stanley J., Maj., ed. *Military History of the American Revolution: Proceedings of the 6th Military History Symposium, United States Air Force*

Academy, 10-11 October 1974. Washington D.C.: Office of Air Force History, Headquarters USAF and United States Air Force Academy, 1976.

Vickery, Paul S. *Washington: A Legacy of Leadership.* Nashville: Thomas Nelson, 2010.

Walsh, Ellard M. Papers. National Guard Memorial Museum, Library, and Archives, Washington, D.C.

Walzer, Michael. *Just and Unjust Wars.* New York: Basic Books, 1977.

Washington, George. *Founders Online,* National Archives, "From George Washington to John Hancock, 25 September 1776," accessed August 21, 2018, http://founders.archives.gov/documents/Washington/03-06-02-0305.
Quoted in Philander D. Chase and Frank E. Grizzard, Jr., eds., *The Papers of George Washington,* Revolutionary War Series, vol. 6, 13 August 1776-20 October 1776. Charlottesville: University Press of Virginia, 1994.

Washington, George. *Founders Online,* National Archives, "From George Washington to John Hancock, 20 December 1776," last modified June 13, 2018, accessed August 21, 2018, https://founders.archives.gov/documents/Washington/03-07-02-0305. Quoted in Philander D. Chase, ed., *The Papers of George Washington,* Revolutionary War Series, vol. 7, 21 October 1776–5 January 1777. Charlottesville: University Press of Virginia, 1997.

Washington, George. *Founders Online,* National Archives, "From George Washington to Robert Dinwiddie, 18 July 1755," accessed August 21, 2018, https://founders.archives.gov/documents/Washington/02-01-02-0168.
Quoted in W. W. Abbot, ed., *The Papers of George Washington,* Colonial Series, vol. 1, 7 July 1748-14 August 1755. Charlottesville: University Press of Virginia, 1983.

Washington, George. "State of the Union". Presidential address, Federal Hall, New York, NY, January 8, 1790. Accessed April 3, 2019. https://www.archivesfoundation.org/documents/george-washingtons-first-annual-message/.

Washington, George. *The Writings of George Washington.* Vol. V, 1776-1777. Accessed July 27, 2018. http://oll.libertyfund.org/titles/washington-the-writings-of-george-washington-vol-v-1776-1777.

Whitley, Edward and Rob Weidman, eds. "The Vault at Pfaff's, An Archive of Art and Literature by the Bohemians of Antebellum New York." Lehigh University. (Accessed July 15, 2018). https://pfaffs.web.lehigh.edu/node/54195

Zengerle, Joseph. "The U.S. military is great on STEM. It should also be great on liberal arts". *The Washington Post Online,* October 3, 2016. Accessed February 13, 2019. https://www.washingtonpost.com/posteverything/wp/2016/10/03/the-u-s-military-is-great-on-stem-it-should-also-be-great-on-the-liberal-arts/?utm_term=.f958af170340

Recommended Further Reading

"About ESGR: Who is ESGR?" Employer Support of the Guard and Reserve, accessed March 7, 2019, https://www.esgr.mil/About-ESGR/Who-is-ESGR

Ackley, Charles Walton. *The Modern Military in American Society*. Philadelphia: The Westminster Press, 1972.

American Civil Liberties Union. *The National Guard and the Constitution, an ACLU Legal Study*. New York: American Civil Liberties Union, 1971.

Ambrosio, Frank. *Philosophy, Religion, and the Meaning of Life*. Chantilly: The Teaching Company, 2009.

Baumer, Franklin L. *Modern European Thought: Continuity and Change in Ideas, 1600-1950*. New York: McMillan Publishing Co., 1977.

Becker, Ernest. *The Denial of Death*. New York: Simon & Schuster, 1973.

Bernstein, Richard J.. *Beyond Objectivism and Relativism: Science, Hermeneutics, and Praxis*. Philadelphia: University of Pennsylvania Press, 1983.

Brehm, Philip A. and Wilbur E. Gray. *Alternative Missions for the Army*. Carlisle: Strategic Studies Institute U.S. Army War College, 1992.

Brennan, Joseph Gerard. *Foundations of Moral Obligation*. Novato: Presidio Press, 1992.

Brunkhorst, Hauke, Regina Kreide, and Cristina Lafont, eds. *The Habermas Handbook (New Directions in Critical Theory)*. New York: Columbia University Press, 2017.

Crossland, Richard B., and James T. Currie. *Twice the Citizen, A History of the United States Army Reserve, 1908-1983*. Washington, D. C.: Government Printing Office, 1984.

Delacampaigne, Christian. *A History of Philosophy in the Twentieth Century*. Translated by M.B. DeBevoise. Baltimore: Johns Hopkins University Press, 1999.

Doubler, Michael D. *The National Guard and the War on Terror: Operation Enduring Freedom and Defense Transformation*. Washington, DC: National Guard Bureau, Office of Public Affairs, Historical Services Division, 2008.

Doubler, Michael D. *The National Guard and the War on Terror: Operation Iraqi Freedom*. Washington, DC: National Guard Bureau, Office of Public Affairs, Historical Services Division, 2008.

Ficarrotta, J. Carl. *Kantian Thinking about Military Ethics*. Burlington: Ashgate Publishing Company, 2010.

Gadamer, Hans-Georg. *Philosophical Hermeneutics, 30th Anniversary Edition*. Translated by David E. Linge. Oakland: University of California Press, 2008.

Enger, Rolf C., Steven K. Jones and Dana H. Born. "Commitment to Liberal Education at the United States Air Force Academy." *Association of American Colleges & Universities*, Spring, 2010. Accessed March 4, 2019. https://www.aacu.org/publications-research/periodicals/commitment-liberal-education-united-states-air-force-academy

Heidegger, Martin. *Being and Time.* Translated by John McQuarrie and Edward Robinson. New York: Harper Perennial Modern Thought Edition, 2008.

Heller, Charles E. *TOTAL FORCE: Federal Reserves and State National Guards.* Carlisle: Strategic Studies Institute U.S. Army War College, 1994.

Heller, Charles E. *Twenty-First Century Force: A Federal Army and a Militia.* Carlisle: Strategic Studies institute U.S. Army War College, 1993.

Hobbes, Thomas. *Leviathan.* New York: Penguin Classics, 1982.

Immerman, Richard H. *John Foster Dulles: Piety, Pragmatism, and Power in U.S. Foreign Policy.* London: Rowman & Littlefield Press, 1998.

Livingston, James C. *Modern Christian Thought: Volume 1, The Enlightenment and the Nineteenth Century, 2nd Edition.* Upper Saddle River: Simon & Schuster/A Viacom Company, 1997.

Mahfouz, Judd D. Chief, Strategy Development Branch, NG JS J59-SD, LA ARNG, email message to author, February 26, 2019.

Malone, Dumas. *Jefferson the Virginian.* Boston: Little, Brown and Company, 1948.

Marcus, Jon. "The Unexpected Schools Championing the Liberal Arts." *The Atlantic*, October 15, 2015. Accessed March 4, 2019. https://www.theatlantic.com/education/archive/2015/10/the-unexpected-schools-championing-the-liberal-arts/410500/.

Miles, Donna. "Service Academies Retain Principles. Embrace Change to Train Future Leaders." *US Department of Defense, DoD News*, May 24, 2007. Accessed March 4, 2019. http://archive.defense.gov/news/newsarticle.aspx?id=46133 Nichols, Ashton. *Emerson, Thoreau, and the Transcendentalist Movement.* Chantilly: The Teaching Company, no year given.

Niebuhr, Reinhold. *Moral Man and Immoral Society: A Study in Ethics and Politics.* Louisville: Westminster John Knox Publishing, 2013.

O'Connor III, Charles A. *The Great War and the Death of God.* Washington, DC: New Academia Publishing, 2014.

Sammons, Jeffery T. and John H. Morrow, Jr. *Harlem's Rattlers and the Great War.* Lawrence: University of Kansas Press, 2014.

Sorely, Lewis. "Creighton Abrams and Active-Reserve Integration in Wartime", US Army War College Quarterly, *Parameters*, Summer, 1991.

Van Fleet, Frank C. *The Foundation and Development of the National Guard Bureau.* Washington, DC: Minuteman Institute for National Defense Studies, 2002.

Wills, Garry, *Cincinnatus George Washington and the Enlightenment.* Garden City: Doubleday &Company, Inc., 1984.

Wolff, Robert Paul, ed. *Kant: Foundations of the Metaphysics of Morals.* Indianapolis: The Bobs-Merrill Company, Inc.,1969.

Index